INSIDE THE TROUBLED ORGANIZATION

# UNSTABLE AT THE TOP

# INSIDE THE TROUBLED ORGANIZATION
# UNSTABLE AT THE TOP

Manfred F.R. Kets de Vries
and Danny Miller

NAL BOOKS

**NEW AMERICAN LIBRARY**

NEW YORK AND SCARBOROUGH, ONTARIO

Copyright © 1987 by Manfred F. R. Kets de Vries and Danny Miller

Published simultaneously in Canada by The New American Library of Canada Limited.

 NAL TRADEMARK REG. U.S. PAT. OFF. AND FOREIGN COUNTRIES
REGISTERED TRADEMARK—MARCA REGISTRADA
HECHO EN CHICAGO, U.S.A.

SIGNET, SIGNET CLASSIC, MENTOR, ONYX, PLUME, MERIDIAN and NAL BOOKS are published *in the United States* by NAL PENGUIN INC., 1633 Broadway, New York, New York 10019, *in Canada* by The New American Library of Canada Limited, 81 Mack Avenue, Scarborough, Ontario M1L 1M8

Library of Congress Cataloging-in-Publication Data

Kets de Vries, Manfred F. R.
   Unstable at the top : inside the neurotic organization / Manfred
F.R. Kets de Vries and Danny Miller.
      p.   cm.
   ISBN 0-453-00562-4
   1. Organizational behavior.   2. Industrial organization.
I. Miller, Danny.   II. Title.
HD58.7.K475   1988
158.7—dc19                                                  87-23182
                                                                CIP

Designed by Gene Gardner

First Printing, January, 1988

1  2  3  4  5  6  7  8  9

PRINTED IN THE UNITED STATES OF AMERICA

# Contents

# Acknowledgments

In the course of rewriting and editing this book a number of people were extremely helpful in stimulating our thoughts and giving critical comments. To one group of helpers, who must be kept anonymous for reasons of discretion, we owe perhaps the greatest debt. We refer to our clients, who had the courage to face their problems and in the process managed to teach us a great deal by asking incisive questions.

We would also like to name a few individuals who encouraged us as we moved along with this project. We are particularly grateful to Sudhir Kakar, Joyce and Lawrence Nadler, Martine and Philippe Haspeslagh, Susan Schneider, Robert Dick, Morris Miller, Victor Levin, William Rodman, Jay Conger, and John Engellau for their thoughtful reading of the draft manuscript or parts thereof and for their many helpful suggestions. We also deeply appreciate the inspired editorial help of Sophia Acland.

Helene Schieder took good care of the final draft, Evelyne Exbrayat, and Barbara Litwak did the typing, and Henriette Robilliard managed the process with her usual efficiency and geniality. For this our deep-felt appreciation.

In addition, Manfred Kets de Vries would like to thank his students at INSEAD, whose reactions to parts of the book were extremely helpful in giving it a focus. Needless to say, they are responsible for only the virtues and none of the vices of what follows.

Finally, we are indebted to Elisabet Kets de Vries and Doe Coover for their assistance in getting this project off the ground.

Manfred F. R. Kets de Vries
Paris, France


Danny Miller
Montreal, Canada

# Special Acknowledgment

We owe a special debt of gratitude to our friend and colleague, Ken Lizotte, contributor to *Cosmopolitan, Business Today,* and many other journals and co-author of *High Inside,* who helped shape our ideas into a prose style we hope the reader finds both entertaining and informative. Ken not only contributed to the writing and editing of the manuscript's many drafts but also brought to the undertaking the sort of patience, creative insight, and dedication that made the work a joy throughout.

# Introduction

Successful organizations frequently attribute their triumphs to the foresight, intelligence, and calculation of their executives. Problems, on the other hand, are blamed on carelessness, error, or plain stupidity. In truth, both these explanations—based as they are on the assumption that managers are perfectly rational beings—often miss the mark.

They miss the mark because corporate executives, like the rest of us, are *not* always entirely rational beings. Executives may, like anyone else, be driven by powerful, entrenched emotions, by aspirations, or by fantasies that can dramatically, and seemingly irrationally, influence the way they run their companies day by day. How often have we seen the imprint of the top manager's personality reflected in the strategies, structures, and cultures of his or her organization. And when the personality is unsettled, chances are the organization will be as well.

The aim of *Unstable at the Top* is to show just how certain aspects of a CEO's personality can affect his managerial style and contribute to the decline—sometimes temporary, sometimes not—of his organization. We identify five very common problematic management styles and trace their roots as well as their consequences. Then we proceed to show how these can be identified, combatted, or avoided. A major premise here is that detection is at least half the cure.

Chapters 2 through 6 identify our five most common "neurotic" organizational types, all of which relate closely to five common problematic personality styles in CEOs. We label our five styles Dramatic, Suspicious, Detached, Depressive, and Compulsive.

In this book we investigate the four major elements of each style: the *personality* characteristics of the CEO; the *structure* of the organization, including the distribution of responsibility and authority, procedures, rules and information systems; *corporate culture* as it is revealed by shared managerial norms, goals, perceptions, emotions, and fantasies; and *strategy* and *decision making*, particularly in the areas of product market strategy, risk taking, adaptation, and innovation.

Many readers will be tempted to try to identify their own firms and leaders among those described in the book. After presenting our five problematic types, we give you a chance to do just that. Chapter 7 aids the detective work by presenting an unlabeled company from the point of view of a new employee. After diagnosis you are challenged to improve things, to find a "cure." Thus our aim in Chapter 8 is to illustrate the obstacles to cures so that you can once again identify any that apply to your own firm. We also hope to draw the fine line between a battle worth fighting and a battleground worth fleeing. And finally, in Chapter 9, we present a disguised case study of a consulting assignment to show how we tried to restore health to a troubled corporation. We offer this chapter not so much as a prescription for managers but rather as a demonstration of the considerable difficulties of turning an organization around.

Because of the confidentiality required when dealing with the emotions, psychological vulnerabilities, and biases of top executives, all examples taken directly from our consulting experience are disguised. However, to make this book more interesting and relevant, we have also discussed as examples certain well-known organizations and executives who have found themselves in the limelight. We have used information reported in the press and in business journals to illustrate the various possibilities and dimensions of our five problematic types. Thus, in numerous cases we discuss company stories and individual histories with which the reader is probably already familiar. Note, however, that we have never met any of these executives, or had any direct association with their companies. Our research has been culled from detailed book histories, articles, and features in such publications as *Fortune* or the *Wall Street Journal*. That we have used secondary sources, and not the actual verbalizations, dreams, fantasies, behavioral patterns, or observations of executives (which is very different from what happens in a clinical setting), means that our examples are not clinically conclusive. All we claim is that documentation found easily in the public record—interviews with CEOs and other corporate managers, policy pronouncements, actual organizational actions, and decisions—suggests a certain CEO mentality which, in turn, seems to be mirrored by the organization. Only occasionally does the sum of the documentation fall neatly into one of the "neurotic" styles we have defined.

The firms and executives discussed in our examples do not by any means illustrate all the characteristics we have summarized under each style. We selected examples only to illustrate specific individual traits as reported in the business literature. Articles and books written about these executives often emphasize particular patterns that illustrate *selected aspects* of managerial styles and corporate syndromes, those that we have isolated independently in our earlier research.*

---

*Readers who wish to pursue "treatment" for their organizations are referred to our book *The Neurotic Organization*, (San Francisco: Jossey-Bass, 1984). The empirical evidence for the typology of unhealthy firms is taken mostly from Danny Miller and Peter H. Friesen, *Organizations: A Quantum View*, (Englewood Cliffs: Prentice Hall, 1984). Of additional help to the reader are the following: Manfred Kets de Vries, ed., *The Irrational Executive*, (New York: International Universities Press, 1984); Kets de Vries, *Organizational Paradoxes: Clinical Ap-*

We must admit to a clear leadership bias. From our point of view, organizations are heavily influenced by their leaders. At the same time, we do not wish to sound dogmatic. Each organizational situation can be driven by many things. Economic factors, competition, or new technologies can have profound impacts. Thus, whether leaders create their organizations, or organizations create their leaders is open to debate. Although we tend to emphasize the first influence, we in no way wish to deny the second.

Throughout the book we frequently simplify matters for purposes of presentation. Our five "ideal types" are really just analytical tools, as are the "pure" styles of management and organization. Many organizations, in fact, are hybrids of one or more of our styles. Most managers of troubled firms, too, display behavior from several categories. We ask you to keep this in mind.

At the same time, remember that our five types are neither arbitrary nor used lightly. They are based on a systematic empirical study of organizational pathology and a thorough examination of managerial, leadership and clinical literature.

One final note. The focus of *Unstable at the Top* is mainly unhealthy firms and factors contributing to their failure. The situations we describe are unstable in more than one way. They tend to be transitory episodes in a company's history. Most organizations have enough vitality to bounce back. In fact, problems might become turning points leading to organizational renewal. The threat of failure often becomes an impetus for future success.

Our framework applies mainly where decision making power and initiative reside largely in the chief executive. But in healthy organizations, and where power is dispersed, a mixture of personalities contributes to decision making. Consequently, in such cases there tend to be fewer extremes, less uniformity in culture, structure, and strategy, and as a result, fewer problems.

---

*proaches to Management* (London: Tavistock, 1980); and Abraham Zaleznik and Kets de Vries, *Power and the Corporate Mind*, (rev. ed. (Chicago: Bonus Books, 1985).

INSIDE THE TROUBLED ORGANIZATION

# UNSTABLE AT THE TOP

---— Chapter One ---—

# Organizations in Crisis

Charles B. "Tex" Thornton was a charming man. Charlie Litton, president of an obscure microwave-tube company in San Carlos, California, doubted Thornton's prospects, however. Yet on a sunny California afternoon in 1953, Thornton, a former officer with Howard Hughes, strode into Litton's office and put down $1 million in cash on the president's desk. According to an article in *Fortune* magazine, Thornton had raised close to $1.5 million to purchase a company that had only slim potential for rewarding the investment. But here he was, cash in hand, meeting Litton's price and eager to take control of the firm.[1]

From that day in 1953 until fourteen years later, Thornton would continue to impress the financial community. In 1954, for example, his new little company, once so obscure, achieved $9 million in sales, an increase of 200 percent from the year before. Four years later, it was averaging close to $100 million a year, and ten years later, $540 million. By the mid-sixties, the once-troubled Litton Industries boasted average yearly sales of $1.8 billion and acquisitions that stretched around the globe. A more inspiring and astonishing success story was hard to imagine.[2]

Reviving a tottering organization, however, was not new to Tex Thornton. He had been the leader in the 1940s of the

1

famous "Whiz Kids," the ten-man systems analysis team credited with introducing modern management techniques into the U.S. Air Force during the war. After the war, many of the team's members joined the Ford Motor Company, where they were instrumental in rescuing it from serious marketing and financial difficulties. As vice-president and assistant general manager at Hughes Corporation from 1948 to 1953, Thornton joined Roy Ash, a Hughes assistant controller, and Hugh Jamieson, a top Hughes scientist, to drive annual sales from $2 million to $200 million.

Thornton, helped by Ash and Jamieson, completely transformed Charlie Litton's small microwave tube enterprise. The nation's business magazines had already picked through many superlatives trying to describe Thornton's character. They noted, for example, that he was a man "possessed of a brilliantly intuitive mind," "the greatest promoter of all time, bar none," "a great, daring ambitious entrepreneur," and "a great dreamer" (read: "visionary"). He was both a dreadful worrier with "varying moods" and a negotiator with "nerves of steel" at the bargaining table. "When he wanted to romance you," one colleague recalled, "he could seduce you without your knowing it."[3] Thornton's affable Texas drawl, his generous smile, and his soft, civilized manner were weapons, the colleague said, for charming your socks off.

Toward the end of the sixties, however, something in the Thornton mystique went awry. In 1968, Litton Industries announced its first ever earnings decline. The firm's stock price plunged 18 points in one week and leveled out at nearly 50 percent below the all-time high set two years before. Net profits dropped, too—drastically—from 63 cents a share to 21 cents, and several Litton divisions showed serious signs of trouble.[4] *The Economist* called it "the anticlimax of one of the most extraordinary dramas in modern American corporate history."[5] *Business Week* named Litton "the dethroned king of the conglomerates."[6] Litton's shipbuilding division alone reported $8 million in excess costs, while other areas suffered sudden, heavy losses from assorted production delays and engineering mistakes.

Thornton and his partners had a hard time accepting this change in fortune. "We do not want to change what we consider the right way to organize just because once in fifty-eight times something happened," Thornton fumed. "There were fifty-seven quarters, after all, when it didn't happen. We will be more alert to signals, but we won't be changing the way we operate. To us, it's not anything." Added Roy Ash, "US Steel was down 31 percent this year and there hasn't been all that much interest."[7] They acknowledged, however, that there might have been some "management deficiencies."[8]

In Litton's case, "interest" in the slump derived at least in part from all the curiosity about the company's prior phenomenal success. Litton's top executives, and in particular Tex Thornton with his aggressive acquisition policies of the late 1950s, had long displayed a verve and brash dynamism that seemed both the theme of America's past and a vision for its future. Litton's managers had homed in on original, futuristic industries—computers, inertial guidance systems, radar, deep-sea exploration, office copy machines, lightweight metal furniture, and electronic calculators. But they had also produced innovations in management techniques that seemed to complement this space-age product mix. Their stock-option plan offered employees significant portions of company equity—more than any other leading firm. Also, engineering teams at Litton followed projects from initial research stages right on through to production, making work more meaningful and satisfying. Thornton and Ash also prided themselves on open-door policies. "Any of our key men," Thornton explained, "can walk into Roy's office or my office at any time."[9] Finally, Jamieson's job, as engineering chief, existed more to coordinate the various project teams than to actually command them. As Ash described it, "We have lots of entrepreneurs at Litton, and this type of person, with his own job security built right into him, does not develop the posture of people in institutional organizations. He does not have to keep things to himself to keep his job. He freely exchanges information laterally."[10] Litton had become a veritable high-tech utopia.

With all this sensitivity to profit, human energy, and the future, how could Litton at that particular time in its history have tumbled so precipitously from its pedestal? If Thornton's radical management techniques fostered such a positive, creative attitude, how could he lose?

In our consultations with top corporate executives, we have encountered situations such as Litton's many times and have observed that, while innovative management and a top executive's personal charisma are usually ingredients of success, these same seemingly positive attributes just as often subvert and sometimes destroy the company further down the road. We label executives like Thornton "dramatic"—a label we will explain in more detail later. Since dramatic executives frequently rely more on personal judgment than on impartial feedback, they too often become overconfident, close-minded, and unresponsive to the ideas and comments of managers and customers, forging ahead with their bold adventures.

"Whose expertise made the company successful in the first place?" dramatic executives reason. Thus even when something does seem to be their fault, they tend not to see this. At Litton, for example, Thornton refused for a long time to reexamine his management style, despite the many advisors who believed strongly that some of his management practices were flawed. As Ernest Stowell, a New York financial analyst, put it, "Was management getting the right information? My answer would be they were not."[11] His criticism suggested that Litton's acquisitions and ambitious new product ideas had ultimately created too much for Thornton to do. Did second-tier managers in their eagerness to please Thornton wax overly optimistic?

Perhaps too little time was spent getting feedback from the marketplace or monitoring the competition. Whatever

Tex Thornton thought Litton should get into was usually tried. With this form of decision-making, serious setbacks were inevitable. Only in the mid-seventies, after an infusion of new top managers, did Litton get out of the slump.[12]

The turn-of-the-century automaker Henry Ford showed throughout a great part of his career many of the characteristics of what we call a "compulsive" manager. Ford wanted complete control of his organization at all times. He was an obsessive perfectionist, a lover of detail. In 1906, he mass-produced the first truly affordable American car, the Model N, for $500. Two years later, he brought out the Model T, a design that sold explosively as soon as it appeared. His idea of making a cheap car for the masses, then an entirely novel notion, made him one of the richest, most successful entrepreneurs in American history.[13]

Because the Model T had been so well received, Ford turned it out year after year with very little change. All energy was directed toward increasing the efficiency of the assembly line. While other auto companies, such as arch rival General Motors, began offering consumers annual style changes and a wide choice of models and colors, Ford refused. He marketed only the Model T for nineteen straight years. During this period, someone asked about the likelihood of offering the Model T in different colors. Ford's oft-quoted reply: "My customers can have any color Model T they like—so long as it's black!"

Ford's authoritarian, do-it-my-way approach had nonetheless served his automobile company well for many years. Continued brisk sales of his Model Ts, in fact, allowed him time to indulge in more private endeavors and leave day-to-day operating matters to others. During World War I, he organized the Peace Ship with fellow pacifists, in the hope that by merely visiting and reasoning with Europeans, he could stop the fighting. The project was a depressing failure and seemed to embitter Ford. As grandson Henry Ford II remarked decades later, "I don't think he ever came out of his cabin, to be honest. . . . The idea was to go over there and stop the war—it was a wild idea."[14]

So after the Peace Ship failed, Ford's pertinacious nature intensified. Increasingly he needed scapegoats when setbacks occurred. He began publicly attacking the Jewish people, using his newspaper, *The Dearborn Independent,* to run virulent anti-Semitic feature articles. One Ford headline read: "The International Jew: The World's Problem."

Also friction began to develop between Ford and the newly organized United Auto Workers union. Ford's compulsiveness now seemed complemented by pervasive suspiciousness—another relatively common dysfunctional management pattern. The automaker decided that unionists, communists, and personal enemies were conspiring against him. Even after General Motors signed a formal contract with the UAW in 1937, Ford refused even to acknowledge the union's existence. Three months after the GM pact was signed, Ford hired goons to beat up the union organizers. Emil Mazey, later secretary-treasurer of the UAW, recalled the incident that has become known as the Battle of the Overpass:

> On May 26 we organized a mass distribution of paper [leaflets and newspapers] in the Ford plant. And [Walter] Reuther, who was a board member of the union, and Dick Frankensteen and about 15 other people were out at Gate 4. Reuther and Frankensteen walked up on the overpass which crossed the street right in front of the plant and the Ford thugs came out and gave them a severe beating. Some carried guns and some had brass knuckles and handcuffs. . . . But Henry Ford Sr. tolerated that kind of violence. He didn't believe in the right of workers to belong to a union or to organize.[15]

A few years later, Ford's developing suspiciousness came to the fore as he targeted the U.S. government as his enemy. He vigorously opposed price controls during World

War II and forbade his executives to meet with government officials. John Kenneth Galbraith, then an administrator with the Office of Price Controls (OPA), remembers that Ford's increasingly chaotic management had created intense anxiety among government officials over his role as a producer of war supplies. "As early as 1941 . . . [Ford's officers] had to slip into the OPA clandestinely," he said, "and many of the discussions we had in '41 and '42 were about whether the Government would have to take over Willow Run."[16] The Willow Run plant, to the concern of government staffers, produced B-24 bombers.

During the war years, Ford's suspicious characteristics slipped over the edge as his fear of enemies took a new turn. In 1943, he used Harry Bennett, an individual long rumored to have had personal connections with the Detroit mob, as his hatchet man. Until that time Bennett had been manager of Ford's River Rouge plant in Dearborn, but he was hardly the typical auto executive. Bennett kept loaded handguns on top of his desk, and all his office windows were fitted with bulletproof glass. Martin Hayden, former editor of the Detroit *News,* remembers, "Bennett was a completely flamboyant roughneck, hired by old Henry to protect the Ford family from kidnappers and that sort of thing. He was stocky, an ex-boxer, rather nice-looking, always wearing a bow tie."[17]

Though never given a formal title such as president or chief executive officer, Bennett ruled Ford Motor Company for the next years with an iron fist, hiring many of his reputed underworld cronies in the process and making them top Ford executives. He was "the kind of fellow," former Michican Governor G. Mennen Williams later told *The New York Times,* "who would never sit anywhere in a restaurant unless his back was against the wall. When I went into his office once, he had a little Webley pistol and he had a target at one end of the room. He would sit at his desk and plug that."[18] Williams added that whenever he paid a visit to Bennett's office or to the Ford plants in general, he always felt as if he were entering a strange new world. Bennett's control of Ford Motor Company terrorized the line workers. Henry Ford II remarked years later that the atmosphere at Ford then resembled a police state: "People were just frightened to death. . . . There wasn't any morale within the company. I think they were probably stealing the place blind."[19]

Finally, in 1946, with the help of his mother and grandmother, the young Henry Ford II wrested control of the firm from Bennett and took hold of the empire his grandfather had built and then virtually destroyed. No accurate records had been kept for many years, dead people were on the payroll, and losses had reached unconscionable heights: $9 million in 1946 alone. Ford, once America's premier automaker, had slipped to a sorry third place in the industry, behind GM and Chrysler.

Here we have a classic example of how the personality of a powerful chief executive, particularly his obsession with control and his unwarranted fear of enemies, almost ruined his company. The CEO's personality dominated the strategy and culture of the company, and the senior Henry Ford's compulsive-suspicious one-two punch nearly destroyed one of history's most successful enterprises.

From the examples of Tex Thornton and particularly of the first Henry Ford, we can see how the behavior of a company's chief executive will have a profound effect on an entire organization. The lack of action on the part of the CEO, however, can have just as damaging results.

The depressive leadership style of Joshua Gordon, president of the Derrigan Corporation (a fictitious name), a manufacturer of plastic products in northern New England, caused serious problems for his staff. One of Gordon's middle managers, a corporate controller named Shirley Taggart, was responsible for tightening Derrigan's financial controls and eliminating production inefficiencies. During her first year on the job, many of her suggestions were adopted to upgrade internal controls.

But in her third year with the company, Taggart began feeling more and more hampered by a sudden lack of access to Gordon. By April, no one at Derrigan had seen Gordon for weeks, either at staff meetings or by private appointment. He'd begun coming to work very late in the morning, closing the door behind him, and taking a lethargic attitude toward events at the company. One day a new rule was instated requiring prior approval before an appointment with Gordon could be scheduled. When Gordon was reached, he tended to be passive, preferring to delay things and decline to approve changes. He displayed great pessimism at times about the prospects for improvement and refrained from taking action.

One day Deborah, Mr. Gordon's secretary, provided some clues to her boss's behavior: "He's going through a very rough time right now. I think it all started when his son got mixed up with drugs a few years ago. Mr. Gordon just has no idea what to do about it. The boy was even arrested late last year and his trial is coming up soon. Mr. Gordon's been very depressed lately, locking himself in his office every day. All business seems to have been put on hold. I've tried talking to him about it, but he won't listen to me. His wife called the other day, too, and poured her heart out, but what could I tell her? I guess all we can do is hang on and hope he gets over this soon and snaps back into shape. That's all I can think of, just wait and see."

Taggart felt sympathy for her boss's plight but didn't have any idea how to help him. Meanwhile, company decisions piled up awaiting his approval. Taggart needed to implement more financial controls, but she couldn't do so without Gordon's assent. Other managers in the different functional areas were also stymied—nothing was happening. Taggart knew if Gordon's depressive attitude went on for much longer, the company was likely to come to a standstill.

Gordon himself seemed to view these events without much concern. A sense of helplessness prevailed in which he deemed it futile to attempt to improve things. We have seen several scenarios like this one. Depressed managers like Gordon see their lives as unsatisfying, perhaps even hopeless. And their organization bears the consequences.

Through our work as organizational researchers, we have uncovered striking similarities between the problematic behavior of executives and the practices of failing or borderline businesses. In such troubled companies, strategy, organizational structure, and culture will often reflect the personality and fantasies of the top manager. We are referring not to whimsical fantasies such as daydreaming but to complex and stable psychological structures that make up a person's inner world and are the building blocks of action.

When a personality has serious quirks, it is often the source of problems that affect the entire organization, particularly when the chief executive holds the balance of decision-making power. The depth of the problems created makes them resistant to change. Simple views of human nature with as catollary the standard quick-fix recommended in current business texts and implemented by management consultants—sophisticated information systems, quality circles, job enrichment programs, divisionalization, strategic business units, decentralization, matrix structures, and so on—are unlikely to be of much help. Often the psychological roots of the problem must be identified so that some form of more appropriate and fundamental corrective action can be taken.

In this chapter, we have tried to give a foretaste of differing styles in executive behavior and how these can affect organizations. We are not suggesting that these unorthodox executive styles always require changing; they may sometimes be quite compatible with a firm's stage of development, industry, and the challenges it faces. But very often they foster a rigidity that inhibits adaptation. In the long run, only a healthy mixture of styles can ensure corporate success.

_____ Chapter Two _____

# The Dramatic Organization

## The Dramatic Executive

**B**y 1970, maverick international financier Bernie Cornfeld had made it to the top. His lucrative Geneva investment management firm, Investors Overseas Services (IOS), had collected $2.5 billion of other people's money in ten short years, and many of his dashing salesmen had become millionaires. Cornfeld reputedly possessed over $100 million, as well as European castles, villas, luxury apartments, planes, boats, fleets of sports cars, and stables of horses. Advisers, employees, valets, and lovely women jockeyed for his attention. It was a life-style consistent with his spirited management style: Cornfeld adored the spotlight.[1]

Central to what we call the dramatic manager's style is a need for grandiosity, which declares: "I want to get attention from and impress the people who count in my life." The dramatic management style mixes aspects of two primary psychological orientations: the histrionic (theatrical, seductive, and showy) and the narcissistic (egotistical and grandiose). Cornfeld embraced both heartily, as a flamboyant speaker and entertainer in public and as a lover of extravagant comforts at home.

13

Cornfeld's life-style created an intriguing executive persona. In his trim gray goatee and finely tailored European suits, Cornfeld offered the money masters of the turbulent sixties and early seventies some measure of vision and prescription. At one presentation, for example, he told bankers and stock analysts about his dream: a more equitable distribution of wealth to everyone willing to participate in economic development within the structure of the free enterprise system. Vietnam, pollution, racism, and other social ills had begun to diminish confidence in the American economic system, he warned. His proposals were at once utopian and revolutionary.[2]

Cornfeld's brash words and confident manner energized his followers. As he denounced the securities establishment and called for personal creativity as a means to wealth, Cornfeld was the embodiment of surprise, imagination—and drama. And his investment concepts sold very well indeed.

The two psychological states integral to a dramatic executive, histrionic and narcissistic, break down into four characteristics: the need for attention; the need for activity; a sense of entitlement; and a tendency toward extremes.

## The Need for Attention.

Dramatic executives seem to crave attention and notoriety. They are inclined to exaggerate their talents and achievements and submit their actions to public scrutiny. They may act as self-appointed messiahs who adopt an emotional cause in order to draw more attention to themselves. While a student at Brooklyn College in 1948, for example, Cornfeld had campaigned for Socialist presidential candidate, Norman Thomas. Much later in life, Cornfeld continued to emphasize social concerns through his money schemes, even as he engaged in questionable financial practices. This angle of social concern, however, helped him gain public attention as the leader of a crusade. He sold himself during the activist years of the sixties as an impassioned financial-political prophet put down on earth to right some key economic wrongs.[3]


## The Need for Activity, Excitement, Stimulation, and Unconventional Risks.

Dramatic executives often lack self-discipline. Their capacity for concentration tends to be limited, and they tire quickly of methodical plans. Instead, their need for constant stimulation results in sporadic innovations that replace organization. Not infrequently these are misguided and unproductive.

In 1982, Oklahoma City's Penn Square Bank went bankrupt, according to analysts, chiefly because of just such unstructured, off-the-mark management behavior. Bill G. Patterson, the bank's thirty-three-year-old senior executive vice-president for oil and gas loans, was suspended from his position just before the bank's closedown because of accusations of irresponsible lending practices. At the beginning of his career, Patterson had earned an enviable reputation for charm and salesmanship. He'd served Penn Square well by reselling many of its loans to larger lending institutions, thus expanding the bank's loan services to its customers.[4]

But his aberrant social behavior became legendary. Nicknamed "Monkey Brain" by classmates at the University of Oklahoma, Patterson had been known during his executive career to drink draft beer from one of his cowboy boots in a public tavern, to initiate food fights in gourmet restaurants in Chicago and New York, and even to show up for work wearing bizarre articles of clothing—a Nazi helmet replete with swastikas one day, Mickey Mouse ears another, and the rags of a hobo on yet another. Such behavior divided his fellow bankers, who either loved his antics or hated them.

Said one former Penn Square associate, "Wherever he went, he seemed to find his counterparts—brash young bankers with more guts than judgment." Their credo, *Fortune* magazine explained, was like that of the new oil barons of the West: "You only go round once in life, so why not do it with gusto!"[5]

The more traditional forces, however, were not amused. An officer from New York's Manufacturers Hanover Trust, present one night at one of Patterson's boot-drinking sessions, uttered to a colleague, "There's no way we'll ever do business with this guy." That summed up the opinions of many bankers.[6]

Patterson exhibited the same eccentricity in his lending practices and his personal style, contributing to Penn Square's financial disaster. The Tulsa *Tribune* reported in 1982 that Patterson personally supervised loans of $115 million to Oklahoma wildcatter Bob Hefner, an amount, *Fortune* added, "grossly exceeding the legal lending limit to one customer."[7]

A former associate of Patterson's explained simply, "His power went to his head." The associate recalled "ego trips," brash statements, and outright lies as the cornerstones of Patterson's career. Patterson, in fact, once boasted to his subordinates, "There are no bad deals. Every deal can be corrected with money." But in correcting such deals, he often misrepresented both plans and resources.[8]

Patterson remained impulsive and unconventional right to the end. On the day of his suspension (pending investigation of his lending practices), he announced to his tellers that it would be all right if they cashed checks for his favorite depositors. Newly approved loans, he assured the tellers, more than covered the balance of these checks. Weeks later, however, investigators discovered that Patterson had once again been merely grandstanding. Cashing favored depositors' checks had created overdrafts at Penn Square Bank of $11 million.[9]

## A Sense of Entitlement

Though dramatic executives often seem generous, warm, and charming, behind their facades may lurk an egotistical and vindictive streak. The textbook dramatic lacks sincerity and is inconsiderate of others. Empathy is often missing, and exploitativeness is common. Dramatic executives frequently take others for granted, causing relationships to be strained and unstable. They see their own ideas and plans as of the utmost importance, certainly more significant than the feelings or notions of others.

We don't want to imply that Patterson or Cornfeld epitomizes this extreme. The latter charmed and impressed his sales recruits and went out of his way to provide them with counsel and fatherly support. On the other hand, one Cornfeld devotee remembers that the man could also be self-centered, pushy, superior, and exhibitionistic: "Cornfeld struck me then—and I saw quite a lot of him for about a year—as one of the most egocentric people I had ever met and I found him irritating. It was inconceivable for him to ever admit that he was wrong about anything. He was always bringing girls around, to show them off, I felt. They were the sort of girls you would expect, highly intellectual Jewish girls, not fashionably dressed, some rather nice. But you felt he just wanted to show them off."[10]

Cornfeld's egocentricity related directly to his tendency to exploit people. After IOS fell apart, the victim of Cornfeld's extravagance and chaotic management, even those who had previously believed in him discovered that he had been misleading them. All those high-minded, messianic declarations about making IOS's employees and investors at once wealthy and socially responsible had not prevented Cornfeld from misrepresenting his investment performance to his customers, engaging in illegal currency transactions, and using large sums of company funds for personal gain. He accepted exorbitant fees for questionable services and lent IOS per-

sonnel large amounts of company cash on whim. Cornfeld
may have felt that his own uses for his customers' monies
served higher purposes than those required by law. Even
after his forced exit, the spectacle continued. After an increasingly bizarre series of events the tottering IOS was
eventually looted by the now-fugitive financier Robert
Vesco.[11]

## Tendency Toward Extremes

Dramatic executives fluctuate between high highs and low
lows, overidealizing something one moment, devaluating it
the next. If fantasies of unlimited power, success, or bril-
liance are cut short, the dramatic leader often lets loose
pent-up feelings of rage, overreacting to seemingly insignificant comments or events. Excessive displays of emotion,
too, can become a trademark.

Take the case of renegade automaker John De Lorean,
who may represent at least this characteristic of the typical
dramatic executive. According to former subordinates, De
Lorean often erupted into rage whenever another colleague
was mentioned in the press. De Lorean also taunted his
employees at times, answering their grievances with the
admonition, "You're making more money here than you've
ever made in your life." He traced employees' phone calls,
too, compiled dossiers on their personal habits, and had
private detectives tail any managers he suspected of disloyalty. As one employee said in an understated way, "It was
not a pleasant, open place to work."[12]

De Lorean's personality illustrates in even more visible
ways this tendency of the dramatic to vacillate between
extremes. In the early seventies, De Lorean underwent a
major personal transformation, during which he abandoned
his secure, ascendant status at General Motors. He had set
records at GM for unit sales and had spent seventeen years

grooming himself—and for a long time being groomed by GM—for the company's presidency. Yet in 1973, he turned his life around.

Once called by a colleague "the squarest guy in the world," the carmaker dyed his graying hair black, had a facelift, grew long sideburns, married a fashion model half his age, and began hanging out in Hollywood. A year later he had even organized his own auto company. The squarest man in the world had become the countercultural entrepreneur, leaving behind his organization-man status to found what he claimed would become the very first "ethical car company."[13]

## The Structure of the Dramatic Organization

Dramatic firms tend to grow and diversify rapidly and haphazardly. But their organization structure lags behind, unable to control and coordinate the many products and broad markets. Also, middle managers in dramatic firms find it almost impossible to adapt to new conditions, since those with the greatest expertise have the least authority. Too much power is concentrated in the chief executive, and too little time is spent scanning the outside marketplace.

Dramatic leaders love meddling in the most routine divisional and departmental operating matters. They often fail to use or even to develop an effective management information system, preferring to do things informally and personally. Executive actions then become the consequence more of the dramatic's intuition than of hard fact-finding.

Itel Corporation, for example, a California leasing company formed in 1967 by Peter S. Redfield, boldly engaged in the risky business of leasing business computers, expensive machine tools, boilers, airplanes, and anything else Redfield and his staff could get their hands on. Concentrating on small- and medium-sized clients and undercutting other leasing firms by wide margins, Itel grew to $1.1 billion in revenues in its first dozen years. By 1979 the company seemed to be facing a highly promising future.

But in the same year, Itel's stock took an unexpected beating, plunging 18 points in the first quarter. In the second quarter, $60 million in losses forced Redfield to resign. Warnings had been there for over a year, but Redfield had chosen not to heed them. Itel's computer orders had already begun to fall sharply months before, the result of speculation that IBM was about to offer more competitive products. Redfield, however, decided the order drop had more to do with Itel's internal problems and forged ahead, confident that the leasing orders would quickly pick up. One colleague remembers Redfield's habit of closing his ears to bad news, enforcing a top-down, limited-information communication system. Thus even when information was gathered by lower-level managers, such managers would usually have too little influence on organizational decisions to permit their knowledge to make any difference.[14]

The company's performance goals, for example, often seemed arbitrary, unrealistic, and determined by fiat. As another Itel official explained, "When we got to a planning session with our calculators, we were told to punch in a 35-percent increase over last year. There was no appeal. My boss just sat there and said, 'Pete needs so many millions from you.' "[15]

Itel's story is one familiar to many dramatic organizations. The company grew much too rapidly for its initial control system to remain effective. Redfield's impulsive acquisitions caused operating problems that took too long to spot, and rapid diversification intensified the firm's already poor internal communication system. By 1979, cost control at Itel had totally broken down. For the first time since its founding, Itel showed overall losses for the entire year. Twenty-five percent of its 6,400 employees had to be laid off, and eighteen of its thirty-two divisions were discontinued.[16] Redfield's exclusive reliance on his intuition had proved inadequate. Itel was caught off guard by the new IBM series. As with Cornfeld and Patterson, Redfield's grandiosity may be partially to blame. Itel's organization had proved too weak to support Redfield's dramatic style of management. It took until September 1983 before Itel finally emerged from chapter 11 bankruptcy.[17]

# Dramatic Culture

In 1955 the young Bernie Cornfeld arrived in Paris as part of a wave of American intellectual exiles. Rather than passing the day on the Champs-Elysées in idle discussion, he began enlisting his bohemian comrades in a movement toward financial gain. Taking his intelligent misfits under his wing, he schooled them in the art of the mutual fund. His tutorials on motivation and initiative represented "an act of liberation," one analyst has said, for his protégés. But it also created a most loyal band of followers for Cornfeld.

Dramatic leaders normally seek and attract exactly the kind of confused, malleable personalities that Cornfeld found in Paris and then transformed. The dramatic leader's action-oriented, grandiose style well suits the dependency needs of such people, permitting them to take up major responsibilities for the organization while subordinating their own needs to those of the leader. Of course, we all have dependency needs, but individuals attracted to dramatic leaders more than most.

Subordinates of dramatic executives tend to idealize their charismatic leaders, ignoring their faults and exaggerating strengths. This idealization may derive from subordinates' feelings of unworthiness. They are therefore unduly flattered even by off-the-cuff remarks of praise from the leader, and devastated by the mildest reprimands. A dramatic leader's subordinates thus permit the executive to wield an excessive amount of control over them through psychological manipulation.

For example, a Cornfeld salesman, Lou Ellenport, spent many years traveling around the world trying to sell mutual funds. He wanted to prove to himself and Cornfeld how good he could be. His odyssey began after he pleaded with Cornfeld to give him an uncharted sales territory. Cornfeld thought about it, then fired off a terse cablegram to Ellenport, who was struggling in a well-worked sales region in Greece. Cornfeld's only three words were: "Go to Libya!"

At the time, in 1961, oil had just been discovered in Libya, so Ellenport did very well there. But his visa expired after three months, leaving him with the urge to show Cornfeld that he could do still more. He roamed through Tunisia, Portugal, England, Turkey, Lebanon, Israel, Saudi Arabia, France, Algeria, Holland, Belgium, the Philippines, Indonesia, and other foreign lands in search of further lucrative sales. Only in Indonesia did he hit the jackpot. Working the embassies, foreign businesses, and oil fields out in the jungle, Ellenport and a second IOS salesman sold $1.5 million of the Dreyfus Fund in nine weeks.

One would assume, after such a Herculean effort, that Ellenport's boss might be waiting to fete and congratulate his stellar performer. And in his own way, this is what Bernie Cornfeld eventually did. Meeting Ellenport in Tokyo, Cornfeld awarded him a Patek Philippe gold watch, praised him, and clapped him on the back again and again.

Then suddenly, Cornfeld asked Ellenport what he planned to do with all of his new money. Ellenport replied innocently that he thought he'd invest it in Fidelity, which was, after all, one of the biggest, most stable investment firms in the United States.

Cornfeld hit the roof. How could his star salesman even consider investing in any firm but Cornfeld's? The Cornfeld company was growing rapidly, getting more stable and profitable every day. He demanded that Ellenport invest his every cent in IOS stock, offering him options on a thousand shares at a cut-rate cost of $21,000. Ellenport gave in. Reflecting years later on Cornfeld's audacity, Ellenport said, "With Bernie you're either the greatest guy in the world or you're nowhere."[18]

Charles Raw, Bruce Page, and Godfrey Hodgson in their book, *Do You Sincerely Want to be Rich?*, gave an account of the turbulent years of IOS: "It was the essence of Cornfeld's achievement that he took confused young men and liberated in them the conviction that, after all, what they sincerely wanted was to be rich. Having done that, he sent them out to comb the world for money. Many years later, an IOS 'workshop session' decided that 'motivation' means 'getting people to want what you want them to do.' It is a manipulator's definition."[19]

Cornfeld's manipulation of his salesman represents exactly the kind of dependent situation dramatic leaders wish to encourage. The dramatic executive expects to be "nourished" by subordinates with confirming—"mirroring" —responses. Not only is conformity demanded, but praise and adulation as well. Cornfeld loved to bask in the limelight of his widely successful personal syndicate, with his lieutenants scurrying about in exotic foreign capitals trying to please him. But even when the business end was taken care of, he still wanted control of his subordinates' lives.

## Sex Symbols

In the dramatic culture, whole worlds revolve around the leader. The hopes and ambitions of other managers in the company center on their idealized top executive. The dreams and desires of these dramatic leaders become the goals and operating plans of the followers with an almost mystical fervor. The leader's very presence can bolster employee initiative and increase morale.

De Lorean, for example, gradually fashioned an executive

image so dazzling it sparked idolization by those both under and around him. Fan clubs arose in the ranks of De Lorean's customers, and in 1982, just before his cocaine arrest, *Fortune* labeled him "the closest thing the auto industry has ever had to a human sex symbol, the kind of man of which legends are made."[20] Like Cornfeld, De Lorean had attained heights heretofore generally reserved for athletes and movie stars.

## Strategy and the Dramatic Executive

Hyperactive, impulsive, venturesome, and dangerously uninhibited—these words describe the strategic characteristics of the dramatic firm. Strategy-makers (here usually only the CEO) live on hunches and quick impressions, skirting facts and detailed analyses, and ignoring both market changes and consumer demand. They address widely disparate projects in random fashion. Power is centralized, preserving the top executive's prerogative to initiate bold ventures independent of anyone else's stabilizing opinions. CEOs can eventually prove to be right in their bold actions, but the reverse is, unfortunately, too often true.

Daniel Ludwig, for example, once a billionaire project engineer, had been a conquistador-like executive all his life. He'd done very well over the years at superprojects that innumerable "experts" had advised him could never be done. In the forties, for instance, he'd constructed a 30,000-ton tanker, twice the size of any earlier cargo ship. In the fifties, he'd dredged Venezuela's Orinoco River. More recently, he established a worldwide cancer research institute with a $14-million annual budget, and attempted a giant tree and rice plantation on four million acres of jungle in Brazil.

"Mr. Ludwig always goes from idea to execution," one of his retired executives explained. "That's how he does everything. It's hit or miss."[21]

Like most dramatic executives, Ludwig was actively involved in the execution of these grand-scale ideas. He believed in neither partners nor shareholders: "100 percent ownership" was his rallying cry.

"I'm a banker's banker," he once commented. "I have $300 million in the bank. Bankers come to me for deposits." He could thus do things his own way.

As if to prove his point, Ludwig spent thirteen years (from 1969 to 1981) trying to make his Brazilian tree farm a profitable venture. For many years, beginning in the fifties, he'd had his subordinates searching all over the world for a suitable tree for a year-round pulp-mill operation in South America. In 1965 he'd settled on the gmelina tree (pronounced without the *g*), a diminutive, fast-growing wood native to India and Burma. His idea, if it worked, was to market the gmelina as pulpwood at prices significantly below anything comparable. To hold down costs, he'd draw on cheap Brazilian labor, taxes, and property (he bought the jungle land for 75 cents an acre), and harvest the product year-round. Ludwig figured such a scheme might yield profits in the area of 30 percent.

His calculations, however, ran aground almost at once. He'd ignored such destabilizing irritations as insects, humidity, erosion, restless workers, conservationists, torrential rainy seasons, cantankerous governments, disease, and poor soil. His advisers began warning that he'd best forget the whole thing. Get out now, they said, the idea just isn't going to work.

Ludwig, however, in his early eighties, wouldn't hear of it. His subordinates obliged him with forecasts that critics attributed to jungle madness. Ludwig lost million after million, erecting an entire town for the native laborers (Monte Dourado, 30,000 inhabitants, with a budget of $6 million a year), and in 1978 he insisted on towing a mammoth pulp mill, built and assembled in Japan, across three oceans and then up the Amazon, a scene that recalls Werner Herzog's movie *Fitzcarraldo*. He also refused to believe World Bank analysts who placed gmelina yields at half his own estimates, and he wouldn't read memos longer than a half a page, not wanting any information, *Fortune* reported, that was not "good news."

Nothing he did worked, so by 1981, after his stubbornness and his feuding with the Brazilian government over land titles and essential services had lost him his billionaire status, he surrendered his beloved 100 percent ownership rule and began seeking investors to help bail him out. Finally, he sold out to a government consortium. By that time, the project was losing $10 million a year and running up debt service charges of $64 million a year. But still Ludwig refused to voice regret. "I came into this world with nothing," he said, "and I might as well leave the same way."[22]

One year later, in 1982, he was rumored to be investigating Paraguay with the curious notion of growing corn on one of its vast arid plains. Forty miles of irrigation ditch would need to be dug to make the scheme work.

Ludwig's visionary schemes had been a key factor in his original success. He was not going to give up, it appeared, after one major setback.

## Created Environments

Daniel Ludwig demonstrates markedly how everything in a dramatic firm seems to flow from the corporate strategies and decision-making style of the dramatic chief executive. Boldness, risk-taking, and diversification are the rule. And instead of reacting to the environment, dramatic executives, often entrepreneurs, create their own personally tailored environments.

In doing so, they place sizable portions of the firm's capital at risk, their frequently impetuous ventures forcing their firms to become highly leveraged financially in order to survive. Strategic moves are often made in the service of grandiosity, with unbridled growth the uppermost goal.

Sometimes the need to be at center stage, to put on a show, reinforces this desire for growth. Many can fall victim to such a need. Roy Ash, chief executive from 1978 to 1981 of Addressograph-Multigraph, a maker of office equipment, had once directed Richard Nixon's Office of Management and Budget. He had also been a cofounder, as you recall from Chapter 1, of Litton Industries.

At Addressograph, however, he finally had a chance to run things all on his own. It seemed to unleash some of his otherwise more dormant dramatic tendencies. Immediately he began to devise many new ideas, hoping to "raise the excitement content" of the sluggish firm. He changed the company name to AM International, took away many of the company's copy machines ("to stop breeding paperwork"), and moved company headquarters from Cleveland to Los Angeles. The last decision was made, he explained, because "Cleveland is not the environment of new frontier technology in electronics. We must place ourselves in a setting where—partly through osmosis—we get a different idea of our future."[23] On the surface, his decisions seemed to signal a bright new beginning, one of promise and zest.

But the expensive move to Los Angeles contributed to AM's financial problems. Other changes alienated the company's long-loyal sales staff, diluted control systems, and used up cash reserves. Ash's acquisitions, for example, seemed exciting but were ill-conceived, and many either went out of business or lost many millions within a year or two of being taken over. Ash also installed a computerized inventory-tracking system that kept delaying production. Turnover, too, ran high (he tried four different presidents in three years in one key division), and in some divisions Ash enlarged the marketing staff without good reason.[24]

By 1981, industry analysts concluded that Roy Ash had been putting up a "skyscraper on sand." AM's debt had risen over 20 percent, inventories had climbed, and production foul-ups and executive resignations had become routine. In spite of all Ash's good intentions, AM simply could not provide the profit to support its changes in procedure or new subsidiary firms.

In February 1981, Ash was dethroned. When the news reached Wall Street, AM stock leaped briefly upward $4 a share, as if to taunt the ex-chief officer. The business press even resurrected a temporarily dormant put-down of Addressograph, applied mercilessly to the company before Ash came aboard:—"Addressogrief-Multigrief."[25]

We can see from the example of Roy Ash and Addressograph that strategy in dramatic firms is frequently inconsistent, unintegrated, and misguided. Ventures undertaken are often uncomplementary, action becomes action for action's sake, and the level of risk-taking climbs. To complicate matters, a dramatic leader's decision-making style tends to be unreflective. Decisions of Daniel Ludwig's, for example, seem to have been made impulsively. The dramatic's hunches and impressions tend to squeeze out all unwanted interpretations or facts. In many instances only views supporting the leader's own are permitted to be heard.

Alfred Sloan, former chief executive of General Motors, relates a story about his dramatic predecessor, Will Durant, the company's founder, who had a penchant for exhibiting elements of this very style. Sloan recalls that when GM executives were contemplating a new corporate headquarters back in 1920, many long, analytical meetings passed without decision as the company's planning staff pored over detailed maps of downtown Detroit, trying to determine the best location. At one of these meetings, Sloan remarked that perhaps an uptown location might be of more benefit since there was less traffic there and the area was that much closer to the company's sales office. Durant replied at once that the idea sounded intriguing. They should go up there one day, he said enthusiastically, and look over a site. In his book *My Years with General Motors,* Sloan describes the day he and Durant finally did:

"I can see Mr. Durant now," Sloan wrote. "He started at the corner of Cass Avenue, paced a certain distance west on West Grand Boulevard past the old Hyatt Building, then he stopped, for no apparent reason, at some apartment houses on the other side of the building. He said that this was about the ground we wanted, and turned to me and said, 'Alfred, will you go and buy these properties for us and Mr. Prentis will pay whatever you decide to pay for them.' I wasn't in the real estate business. I didn't even live in Detroit. But I went ahead."[26]

This purchase did not end Durant's guesswork, however. When Sloan announced to Durant that the half-block he'd requested was now theirs, Durant told Sloan to go back out and purchase the other half. There was no discussion, analysis or reflection—just action!

"I don't know that he intended to use all of it immediately," Sloan recalls, "but it was soon used. The General Motors Building which was built there started a new business district in Detroit."[27]

Sloan's recollections of Will Durant's impulsiveness illustrate the dramatic manager's aversion to consulting with subordinates or staff experts, even when making critical business decisions. Participative policy-making and consultation are not common among dramatic strategy-makers. Their major ventures are most often initiated on the basis of one point of view, their own, compounding the danger that decisions could prove disastrous. Ultimately, Sloan had to take over GM to rescue and consolidate it after the excesses of Durant's regime.

# Strengths and Weaknesses
## of Dramatic Organizations

## Strengths

Bernie Cornfeld brilliantly lit fires under his sales staff, radically transforming them into hard-driving investment-fund salesmen. Before many of his recruits realized it, they were making money. He had got them, and his business, moving. Peter Redfield was a similarly dynamic force when he founded Itel: He possessed the flair and confidence necessary to motivate a new company entering a risky business. Dramatic executives are in fact usually highly successful at creating the momentum to take their businesses through the start-up phase.

Their creativity can also continue to propel them well after this phase is accomplished. De Lorean and Cornfeld, for example, built up astonishingly impressive empires before their dramatic styles caught up with them. And though Ludwig's Brazilian debacle eroded his billionaire status, the boldness that directed his life created that wealth. Redfield, too, though he left Itel in defeat, rebounded just one year later as the head of four much smaller but vibrant and respectable manufacturing concerns.

As well as harnessing their energy to launch new businesses, dramatic executives often come up with good ideas for revitalizing existing firms that are tired or failing. Roy Ash got Addressograph moving in the beginning. His style of management gave his assessments an initial boost. He labeled his ideas "a deliberate attempt to change a corporate culture." Stressing more profitable products and recruiting more youthful managers, he pushed the company out of the red for the first time in a decade in his first year at its helm, pushing up the value of AM shares by 55 percent.

It is not unusual, of course, that dramatic executives do succeed. One of the more consistent examples of dramatic success has been Occidental Petroleum's Armand Hammer. His first dramatic venture was initiated back in the twenties, falling upon him quite by chance. At that time, while vacationing in Russia, Hammer happened to meet the new Russian leader, Vladimir Lenin. During their meeting, they discussed various potential East-West transactions, including trade agreements and construction projects. Hammer was not even a businessman at the time, but a young physician about to begin an internship. However, by the time he left Russia nine years later, in 1930, he had forgotten all about medicine. He and Lenin had arranged enough exclusive business deals to make Hammer a very wealthy, and influential, new American tycoon.

In the next twenty-five years, Hammer increased his power and resources by purchasing many small enterprises and investing in works of art. Then, in 1956, he bought a few thousand shares of stock in Occidental Petroleum, at the time a struggling young oil-drilling concern. Occidental's net worth in the mid-fifties stood at only $100,000. Today the company is worth many billions.[28]

Hammer now owns 1.2 million shares of Oxy's stock, and until 1978 served as the company's president. He rules the company from his perch as CEO and board chairman, and his inspired deals over the years are credited with making the company the major enterprise it now is. One gamble back in 1961, then termed "Hammer's Folly" even by Hammer's own directors, led to major oil finds in Libya that dramatically increased Occidental's profits.

A steady streak of luck may have made the difference for Hammer. His command of details and vast knowledge of the business, complemented by his extensive political connections, certainly helped to improve his chances of success. He often also engaged in highly unorthodox, impulsive management practices, but in his case we can see how this style can sometimes work.

Hammer's victories over the years, as well as his irascible attitude, have created a popularity and cult status for him that has never diminished. One Occidental annual report, for example, was emblazoned with a vivid four-color portrait of Hammer: "a one-man flying entrepreneur." There are few large companies so identified with one man. And over the years, stockholders, directors, employees, and industry analysts have registered generally unanimous approval of Hammer's methods, personality, and style, in spite of, or perhaps because of, his legendary elimination of dissenters.

"There's not a deal made in this company that I have not made," Hammer once bragged, listing diplomats, presidents, cabinet officials, and even a pope as those with whom he has negotiated. "I'm the chief executive and I intend to remain as long as God will permit me."[29]

This kind of bravado and undeterrable forward motion keeps Hammer and other executives like him always in the running. Dramatic executives can't conceive of management, and indeed life, any other way. But most dramatic executives are neither as brilliant nor as lucky as Hammer.

## Weaknesses

A major weakness of the dramatic firm is its lack of a consistent strategy. Itel's octopuslike acquisitions, for example, made its true objectives and focus hard to pin down. As one stock analyst said after the fall, "To my knowledge, no analyst ever really knew what the company did." Redfield's constant expansion programs had fashioned Itel into a sprawling, chaotic conglomerate with neither strategy nor adequate control.

Rash expansion policies also cause resources to be squandered. Roy Ash's determination to move AM's location and his many acquisitions rocked the firm's financial foundations. Cornfeld, meanwhile, allowed his personal vision and the growing acclaim he was receiving to blind him to the fact that he could not do everything himself. In the spring of 1970 his empire finally collapsed, unable to withstand the tremendous strains put on its resources by overexpansion. Still Cornfeld was reluctant to admit that his strategies weren't working.

In a widespread operation, control and profitability may be more difficult to achieve than the dramatic executive realizes. Daniel Ludwig, who undertook his Brazilian tree farm adventure as yet another in a string of complex international projects, failed to monitor and research it adequately. It ran wild, draining him personally of millions of dollars in resources and over a decade of unprofitable time. Ludwig's stubborn refusal to let go of his dream amplified the problem.

A final weakness relates to the dramatic executives' relationships with their employees. Their grandiose designs rarely leave room for much consultation with, or feedback from, the second-tier managers. Ash, for instance, insisted on "immersion management" and personally dissected even the most minor details of matters perhaps better attended to by subordinate experts. Participative decision-making was something he neither encouraged nor expected could substantially help; he habitually refused feedback. The inadequate role of second-tier managers in a dramatic organization means vital information may never reach the CEO; capable managers will be driven away by frustration and their places taken by uncreative yes-men.

## Chapter Three

# The Suspicious Organization

## The Suspicious Executive

From 1924 until his death in 1972, J. Edgar Hoover dominated the Federal Bureau of Investigaton with his deep suspicion, hypersensitivity, and never-ending readiness to repel any threats to his authority. The FBI under Hoover became less an agency for diplomatic detective work and more a crime-related war department, an entity all its own, complete with battle strategies, secret campaigns, and refined intelligence systems.

Hoover started it all. The FBI had been vigorous and aggressive even before he became director, rounding up draft dodgers after World War I, breaking strikes and Ku Klux Klan rallies during the Harding administration, and compiling dossiers on over two hundred thousand "suspected Communists" in the early twenties. But it was Hoover, as the bureau's assistant director, who had overseen these operations. In fact Harding's attorney general, A. Mitchell Palmer, was eventually to comment on how impressed he'd become with young Hoover's "great zeal" and "distrust of all things foreign." As the years went on, this same zeal and consummate distrust were to become both the Bureau's and Hoover's trademarks.[1]

J. Edgar Hoover possessed, by our definition and criteria, many of the characteristics of the suspicious-style executive. Of course, we may wonder if a successful FBI chief could be anything other than this, given the nature of the "business." The question remains, however, did he have to go as far as he did?

Hoover's guiding vision, like that of all suspicious-style executives, might have been: "Some menacing superior force is out to get me. I had better be constantly on my guard. I cannot really trust anyone." Over a career that spanned nine presidential administrations and almost fifty years, Hoover mined this theme by exhibiting every one of the traits we commonly associate with executives having a suspicious disposition. These include:

1. *Vigilant preparedness to counter any and all attacks and personal threats.*

Hoover spent a lifetime battling the "Red Menace" (his notion of monolithic communism set on taking over the world), as well as subordinates who doubted him and superiors, such as Attorney General Robert Kennedy, who challenged him.

2. *Hypersensitivity.*

Hoover was "finicky as hell about neatness," one of his former agents has said, and about violations of even the most picayune rules and regulations. Even slight errors or off-the-cuff remarks could cause an agent's transfer, suspension, or firing without warning.

3. *Coldness and lack of emotional expression.*

"Hoover had an ability to keep you at arm's length," a former agent has said. The coldness extended, too, to a generally watchful, reserved, precise, and calculating personality. While suspicious-style executives occasionally have volcanic tempers, they usually don't display much emotion. Hoover could get upset and angry over the smallest threats, but otherwise he seemed to suppress joy, depression, sadness, and compassion.

4. *Deep suspicion, distrust, and insistence on loyalty.*
Loyalty was almost sacred to J. Edgar Hoover, so fearful and doubtful was he of the sincerity of others. One agent remembers hearing Hoover talk about loyalty and "what a terrible thing" disloyalty was. He recalled also a time when one of Hoover's assistant directors (in charge of public relations for the FBI) tried to calm the director after an editorial in the *Washington Post* had viciously attacked one of the bureau's investigations: "I said to the director, 'Mr. Hoover, if I had known that they were going to print those subversive, Communist-inspired lies about you, I would have gone over there and hurled myself bodily into the presses."
Hoover later commented to friends gleefully, "He may not be very smart, but nobody can doubt his loyalty."[2]

5. *Overinvolvement in rules and details to secure complete control.*
Hoover could always find a rationale for the introduction of new rules. He created the bureau's "Manual of Rules and Regulations," a compendium of modes of personal conduct of baroque origins that, if not followed to the letter, could easily end one's career. Given his overconcern for hidden motives and special meanings, Hoover was, in fact, obsessed with details and regulations. Though much of his career was spent in tracking important criminals or keeping a wary eye on the worldwide Communist front, Hoover could also be counted on to enact astonishingly picayune directives merely because some trivial incident had upset him. One former agent recounts a story of Hoover being driven through the streets of Washington in his limousine. Another vehicle suddenly banged into the left side of his car as both tried to make a left turn. From that moment on, Hoover never again sat behind his driver. He ordered that henceforth there would be "no left turns" taken at any time when he

was a passenger. Movements to the left, he decreed, must be made by turning right, then right again, right once more, then proceeding two blocks down to the street in question and turning right once again.[3]

Hoover prided himself on the notion that he personally attended to all the details. Once an agent implied that since the FBI had got so big, neither Mr. Hoover nor any one man could any longer "keep track" of everything. "I want you to know . . ." Hoover retorted, swelling up like a toad, "I still personally keep track of everything that goes on in this Bureau!"[4] Hoover's voice rose as he responded to the man, growing more and more agitated.

### 6. *Vindictiveness and overreaction.*

The following incident demonstrates how vindictive Hoover could be when someone antagonized him. He had just overheard a TWA pilot criticize the FBI's handling of a hijack case. Angry at the comments, he issued an official order forbidding all bureau agents to book any further flights on TWA. He dispatched a similar order, too, regarding the Xerox Corporation after becoming angered by their lack of cooperation during the investigation of a case. Xerox machines were subsequently removed from all bureau offices.

### 7. *A craving for information.*

The craving for information is a strong and fundamental impulse that is extensively manifested in the structure of suspicious organizations. Hoover wanted to know precisely what every field agent was doing: how much time was spent in the office, and the overtime done by each agent. Every tidbit of information about public officials—including rumors and vague accusations—was methodically catalogued and kept by Hoover in his personal office for ready reference.

# The Structure of the Suspicious Organization

## The Quest for Details

Suspicious-style executives want their organizations to be like themselves: always alert and ready to fight. Thus, the main characteristics of their organization's structure are organizational intelligence gathering and controls, abundant analysis, and centralization of power.

Suspicious executives are victims of their own feelings of persecution. Many of them have reactive, bunker mentalities—they are always on the defensive—which pervade their organization's structure, culture, and strategy. Information is the central power resource of the suspicious executive. The more information he or she has, the more he or she feels prepared to counter the threats of others. Sophisticated information systems—the institutionalization of suspicion—are then developed to identify potential threats from government, competition, or consumers. Budgets, costs centers, profit centers, and elaborate cost-accounting are all incorporated to control the internal workings of the company. Perpetual vigilance is an important theme, as is readiness.

Traces of the kind of internal information gathering we feel is characteristic of suspicious executives seem to be found in the management style of former ITT president Harold Geneen. For many years Geneen was a legend in the corporate world for his superhuman concentration and ceaseless personal energy, as well as for the fine rate of growth at ITT during his eighteen years as chief executive. During his reign, he consolidated a disorganized, somewhat unambitious telecommunications network, whose business could be found chiefly in small countries outside the United States, into a great conglomorate, all the while believing, with an almost religious fervor, the suspicious executive's maxim: Information is power.

Geneen became famous, for example, for his once-a-month, three-day-long staff meetings, always held at the corporate headquarters in New York and the European head office in Brussels. These required onerous homework assignments for his already overworked top executives. It was necessary to study—almost memorize—voluminous reports from every profit-and-loss division, however small, in the entire company in preparation for the big monthly meeting. Geneen wanted to have every last detail and he wanted each one examined, challenged, and analyzed by his men. He even required similar monthly exhaustive airings of every problem and goal at lower echelons, plus annual reviews of each division's business plans and revised five-year forecasts.[5]

"If I had enough arms and legs and time," Geneen once remarked, "I would do it all myself."[6] As a workaholic, he tried. But since he could not, he demanded instead that everyone's business be brought to him directly and dissected in his presence. Financial controls were the key, he believed, to his profits. But these were enforced only by communicating each "unshakable fact," and by mercilessly and endlessly scrutinizing divisional plans and problems. As Geneen would say, "I don't believe a man's opinion until I believe his facts."[7] He has been called "the Grand Inquisitor."

Harold Geneen thrived on exhaustive days-long regular meetings and on his copious information systems and controls. He maintained an intricate, extensive spy network of four hundred "checkers" whom he sent around at random to scrutinize all ITT companies and divisions and to double-check each fact and detail, in order to see whether something not covered in the regular reports might be going on. Geneen, in fact, was given to sometimes frightening displays of anger if some matter, however minute, was discovered during these inspections that he felt should have been brought up previously at one of his meetings. Geneen's systems were designed to ensure both thorough information gathering, the first characteristic of the suspicious organization, and abundant, exhaustive analysis, the second.[8]

Similarly, so extensive and zealous was Hoover's centralization of FBI information that even today his agency remains indispensable to the nation's local and state police departments. These rely extensively on the FBI's highly sophisticated data in fingerprint files, crime rate surveys, fraudulent check files, "modus operandi" files, lab services and "most wanted" lists. In the introduction to the book *The FBI in Peace and War* by Frederick Collins, Hoover himself said: "Imagine if you can 300,000 square feet of space cases containing the life histories of millions of people. There has never been anything like it before in the history of mankind. Yet, by an ingenious system which has proved a lifesaver in these days of incredibly quick expansion, the Bureau's trained personnel can identify any incoming fingerprints in less than three minutes if a previous record is on file in these miles of metal cases."[9]

## The Hoarding of Power

Another trait of the suspicious organization—extreme centralization of power—is perhaps best illustrated by the Hunt brothers of Texas. Nelson Bunker Hunt, who once claimed "a billion dollars isn't what it used to be," and his brother, William Herbert Hunt, may be the world's most opulent pair of siblings. They are perhaps best known for their failed attempt to control the world supply of silver. Their empire, inherited from their poker player/oil baron father, stretched from the oil derricks of one of the largest American oil firms, Placid Oil, to the world's biggest privately held drilling contractor, Penrod, and the largest American beet-sugar refinery, Great Western. In their heyday it encompassed millions upon millions of acres of developed and undeveloped real estate, one thousand thoroughbred racehorses, 2.5 million tons of coal reserves, the Kansas City Chiefs football team, full ownership of the World Championship Tennis circuit, four hundred Shakey's Pizza outlets, four million acres in Australia, major allotments of the Louisiana Land and Exploration Company, Global Marine (owner of the ship *Glomar Explorer*), Gulf Resources and Chemical Company, and a large number of Dallas restaurants and hotels.[10]

Yet this vast, almost incomprehensible corporate kingdom was controlled directly and entirely, without question, by the brothers themselves. Even their individual company presidents appeared to be little more than figureheads, as one-time Hunt insider William Bledsoe has testified. Before the House Subcommittee on Commerce, Consumer and Monetary Affairs in 1980, Bledsoe explained that the Hunts' maze of interlocking directorships, partnerships, trusts, mergers, and foundations were all tightly controlled by the beneficiaries of the trust estates, namely Nelson Bunker and his brother, and that no policies were ever enacted without the brothers' approval: "I know of no instance where the advisory committee or the trustee of any of these trusts ever made a decision or a recommendation that properties or interests be bought or sold," Bledsoe declared. It was always the Hunt brothers themselves who did the deciding."[11]

The Hunts have dominated or intruded into the most detailed decision-making in a great many of their myriad holdings. Geneen had the need to control all. And Hoover, with his personal identification with the bureau, powerfully enforced his regime of autocratic direction. Hoover, in fact, provides a marvelous example of how a suspicious-style executive can often emerge as the very persona of his organization. After all, Hoover was, and to many people still is, the FBI itself. One observer even commented, "No other agency in the federal government bears the imprint of a single personality as clearly as has the Federal Bureau of Investigation."[12] He was a man who insisted that all bureau activities be performed in his name, and who, as we have seen, strove to cultivate an impression that he personally attended to every detail.

It has been said, too, that when Hoover died, the bureau—the real bureau—died with him. It was the end of an era, and the monument he had so painstakingly built up began to disintegrate and transform.

## Suspicious Culture

The culture of the suspicious firm is often rife with paranoia. In extreme cases suspicion looms everywhere, the atmosphere rankles with distrust, hostility, and defensiveness, and visions of the outside world call up images of "good and bad" and "them versus us." There is also a never-ending vigilance toward significant enemies. Sometimes the suspicion stems from a period of traumatic challenge: A strong market dries up, a powerful new competitor enters the scene, or damaging legislation is passed. Then harm done by any one of these forces may cause the manager to become distrustful, afraid, and convinced of the need for stronger intelligence gathering.

In his *Experiences in Groups*, the psychoanalyst Wilfred Bion labeled such cultures "fight or flight."[13] Fear of attack is on everyone's mind. And although there exists an ever-present readiness to strike out at an enemy or challenge, there sometimes exists an urge to run, hide, or wait out the storm.

FBI agents, for example, were constantly retreating from their boss's eccentricities. Whenever J. Edgar Hoover snapped out an order, his men jumped. Former FBI agent Joseph L. Schott explains in *No Left Turns*:

Under Mr. Hoover, you had to work on the premise that the Director was infallible. If you did not really believe this—and of course most employees certainly did not—you nevertheless had to pay lip service to it to survive. Anyone who ever worked for the Director and who denies that this condition prevailed is either mentally retarded or lying. And, if you were ambitious and desired to rise in the organization, you had to pay a still higher toll in the form of exaggerated sycophantic respect and adulation for him."[14]

Insecurity, then, was the rule, as was dependency. FBI agents climbed upward in rank only by embracing these toadying traits and stifling personal initiative. As one veteran agent recalled:

There was a constant desire on your part to please him. You wanted to obtain that praise from him, that letter of commendation, that incentive award. When you did, you had a great sense of pride in it. It gave you a feeling of exhilaration; you had accomplished something. He had [a way of] making you want to work your guts out for him . . . I rebelled at the idea of working through fear, but I did it anyway. This was my niche. I have always wondered whether the fear was necessary, whether it might have been better to rule on the basis of mutual respect. But it is hard to fight success."[15]

In the truly suspicious culture, the world outside, and sometimes inside, is split into two clearly marked categories: "good," that is, in line with the ideas and beliefs held by dominant members of the particular culture or dominant faction in that culture; and "bad," not conforming to such beliefs. Participants in these suspicious cultures often use this friend-enemy breakdown to deny responsibility for their own actions—to point to the bad guys. They may look to the boss for answers, or retreat from crises and problems as soon as they appear. Personal weaknesses are ignored, and blame is always cast elsewhere for mistakes. Sometimes the accusations fly hot and heavy. In the words of one suspicious-style executive, "Someone out there wants to get us and drive us to defeat. It's certainly not something we did ourselves."

Extreme manifestations of the suspicious culture prevailed at District 1199 of the Hospital and Health Care Employees Union when Doris Turner took control in 1982, amid vitriolic charges of ballot-fixing and death threats, beatings and financial irregularities. 1199's previous president, Leon Davis, a man who created 1199 almost singlehandedly (by organizing pharmacy workers in the thirties), has since diplomatically labeled his designation of Turner as his successor a "mistake." Turner has in turn attacked Davis publicly, implying that he and his clique "hated" her so much they would "destroy the union to get at her."[16]

"Doesn't Moe Foner [a Davis ally] have anything better to do than sit up there in the national union office, planting stories and making up rumors about me?" Turner asked a reporter.

But the infighting and factionalism did not end there. A financial officer stepped forward during litigation involving the feuds and swore that Turner, who is black, told him, "I will never feel safe in my position as president until I get rid of all the Jews who use political power against me in this union." The same officer reported anonymous death threats when he refused to cut off Jewish employees' pay, at Turner's request. Said he:

"They called me a Nazi coward and said they would blow up my home, my car, and my family. I quit my job immediately."

Two years of this kind of warfare dominated the union internally after Turner's election, according to Joe Klein writing in *New York* magazine. It was the national office versus the district, and the casualties came in the form of firings, layoffs, early retirements, and clandestine transfers.

"Some of Turner's loyalists," wrote Klein, "made life very unpleasant for the Davis people who remained." One such loyalist, a white male, explained, "[Doris] was too threatened. For years, she and I had gone into negotiations together, and the bosses—white men—had dealt with me as if she weren't there. I tried to make them realize she was an equal partner. I knew she was resentful. I just didn't realize how angry she was until she took over the union. She stopped paying me. People made death threats. I had to go."[17]

## Advancing the Cause

Suspicious leaders' concerns cause them to maintain and control things very closely. They are careful about whom they hire, whom they reward, and whom they promote. Suspicious leaders want only to advance executives or line managers who reinforce their own views ("good people"). Managers who differ or dissent risk demotion, isolation, or swift, unexpected dismissal.

When Henry Ford II fired Lee Iacocca in the summer of 1978, for example, he did so because Iacocca, in Ford's mind, had begun to go astray. Although Ford's management style cannot be easily classified, Iacocca brought out his suspicious disposition. In Iacocca's view, Henry II grew increasingly threatened by his achievements, particularly after the widespread success of the Iacocca-developed Fiesta, a small, fuel-efficient, front-wheel-drive sedan. The Fiesta had succeeded despite Henry's promulgations about "minicars, miniprofits" and was a particularly big success in Europe. In the aftermath of the sixties, respect for authority and old wealth and stature had declined in the United States. Henry Ford II had therefore been looking more and more to Europe for Old World homage and esteem. Yet now one of his own executives stole the limelight. According to Iacocca, the introduction of the successful, small-scale Fiesta had made Ford, the grand master, look ignorant and dated, especially in Europe, his treasured new milieu.

"He turned animal," Iacocca recalled in his 1984 book, *Iacocca: An Autobiography*. "I imagine his first impulse was: 'I don't want that Italian interloper taking over.' . . . When Henry thought I'd steal the family jewels, he had to get rid of me."[18] And he did, setting the stage with an "audit" of travel and expense accounts of top executives. According to Iacocca, Ford conducted a full-scale investigation of his business and personal life. At the time, top executives in the Ford Motor Company would leave the building to make phone calls, afraid that their offices were being wiretapped. Drapes were pulled down and conversation would take place in hushed tones for fear of the watchful, suspicious Henry II. Finally, in 1978, a surreptitious and insidious erosion of Iacocca's power base took place with the introduction of an "Office of the Chief Executive." Iacocca was obliged to share his decision-making authority with a vice-chairman and a director. Soon Ford accused Iacocca of ganging up on him by going behind his back to outside directors of the company. Said Ford to Iacocca, "Sometimes you just don't like somebody," and with that the latter found himself unemployed.[19]

The suspicious top executive is not alone, however, in deliberating over who should or should not work for the company. Often a suspicious chief executive's pronouncements are simply a trigger for the overly dependent second-tier executives who share the boss's fears and want to see enemies of the organization done away with. A mere word or two from the leader is frequently enough to accomplish this.

"I have been looking over the supervisors at the Seat of Government (Washington, D.C.)," Hoover once announced during a meeting with his highest-ranking bureau officials. "It seems to me a lot of them are clods," he added. "Get rid of them." None of the officials present knew precisely whom Hoover was referring to, yet this was all he really had to say. The officials ran out and instantly created a "Clod Squad" and began witch-hunting bureau supervisors with traits known to be despised by the director, particularly complacency, sloppiness, or loose morals. This, of course, led also to further suspicions among bureau clerks, creating Gestapo-type surveillance tactics in which questionable activities were expected to be reported whenever and from whomever they emerged. This meant lots of "tattling and snitching" among the clerks, Joseph Schott remembers, orchestrated by supervisors and high-level executives who developed stool pigeons to keep up with what was going on.[20]

"The bureau seemed to take a lot of interest in the sexual activities of the clerks," Schott explains. "Allegations of s-e-x activities could get a clerk fired faster than almost anything."[21]

Such an atmosphere leads frequently to depressed morale and petty, unproductive behavior. Since a premium is placed on information as a source of power, divisional executives and departmental and line managers may become reluctant to discuss common problems openly. Giving out too much information, or too much accurate information, might permit one's rival an opportunity to surge ahead. Thus adversary relationships develop, making coordination among segments of the same organization difficult. Secrets abound and a "protect yourself" ethic rules.

Distrust of one's colleagues and social pressure to conform had grown to remarkable proportions in the Hunt organization by 1975. Associates and former employees testified at a trial that year that the Hunts' use of private detectives, bribery, and illegal wiretaps to get, and learn, what they wanted knew no bounds. Although acquitted of a wiretapping charge that year, the Hunts never denied the deed. They didn't realize, they maintained, that wiretapping their own employees was against the law.[22]

On another occasion, Herbert Hunt hired a detective to follow one of his part-time consultants—a man who was not even a regular Hunt employee—who was rumored to be philandering with another man's wife. After many weeks of investigation, the detective and the husband encountered the guilty couple in a North Dallas shopping mall. A shouting match ensued and fists began to fly. The consultant even pulled a gun, pointing it squarely at his assailant. Moments later the two men were rolling around on the pavement, scuffling their way through various department stores, until security guards and store personnel finally pulled them apart.

"Let me go! Leave me alone, let me go!" the detective cried, shaking off the store employees. "I work for Herbert Hunt!" He began waving high the consultant's gun—he had wrestled it away during the fight—and ordered the man to give up his illicit affair. The next day, the incident came out in the press.

In the glow of publicity, Herbert admitted somewhat sheepishly that he had had the consultant followed simply because he didn't enjoy the image of what the man had been doing. "I just don't want someone working for me who's out there playing around," he said. This, he believed, justified his every action.[23]

## Strategy and the Suspicious Executive

We turn now to some common strategies and decision-making approaches of suspicious firms. In general, suspicious executives tend to react piecemeal, responding disjointedly to the moves of competitors, rather than designing integrated unified strategies. In a suspicious organization, a decision may take a very long time to make, due to overabundant analysis, information gathering, and weeks or months of consultation. Suspicious strategy-making carries with it a sizable element of conservatism. Fear often causes an inability to innovate, extend resources, or take risks.

Likewise, if other firms introduce a product successfully, the suspicious firm will probably imitate them. Such a kneejerk orientation impedes the development of a focused and consistent strategy, since the suspicious firm's strategy becomes far too concerned with individual external forces and not nearly enough with its own plans, goals, and unifying programs. Strategies are thus fragmented, wavering, and lacking an integrating theme.

Suspicious firms frequently attempt product diversification to reduce their risk of reliance on any one product. Managers become so wary of being overly dependent on one segment of the market that they may spread themselves too thin and become incapable of developing any distinctive competence. Then, because diversification requires more elaborate control and information-processing mechanisms, it often actually reinforces the firm's concerns about being taken advantage of.

A semiconductor manufacturer we studied three years ago, which we will call Paratech Inc., offers a revealing example of how such a scenario can take place. Its two founders had worked for a much larger electronics firm that did a great deal of top-secret defense contracting. Three factors seemed to contribute to the founders' paranoia:

1. They never forgot an episode at the large electronics firm in which Soviet spies had stolen valuable designs.

2. A competitor regularly seemed to beat the firm to the marketplace with products that Paratech had originally conceived.

3. A high rate of bankruptcy loomed in the semiconductor field.

To counter the first factor, Paratech's two founders took all kinds of precautions to prevent their ideas from being stolen. For one thing, they fragmented jobs and processes so that only a few key people in the company really understood the products. They also almost never subcontracted any of the work, and they paid their employees extremely high salaries to give them an added incentive to stay with the firm. Unfortunately, however, these three precautions placed Paratech's costs among the highest in the semiconductor industry, limiting both their profit margins and resources.

The founders created other problems for themselves. Their minuscule profit margins caused them to hold back on expenditures on research and development, so the competition was regularly able to beat them in the introduction of new products. Also, they scanned the environment too carefully to see what the competition was up to, compiling all the needed data and scouring it in planning meetings that lasted well into nights and weekends. Such lengthy analyses, of course, drove them farther behind, permitting markets for their high-tech products to become saturated. Profits from new inventions were never forthcoming, and one opportunity after another passed them by. Ultimately, Paratech's profits dwindled to nothing, making it one of the least successful semiconductor firms in an often lucrative industry.

## Strengths and Weaknesses of Suspicious Organizations

### Strengths

A suspicious executive usually has a good knowledge of events inside and outside the firm, and this may be seen as a strength. Excellent information systems can inform managers of key threats and opportunities and put them in the best position to counter them. This applies equally well to the CEO on a personal level. Hoover, for example, remained in charge of the FBI because he always knew exactly what was going on. When Richard Nixon tried to convince him to retire in the early seventies, he countered by telling the president that he would retire only if Nixon would say that he was hurting his administration.[24] Since Hoover was so enormously popular with the public (a master of the media), and probably was also familiar with the dirty linen of many politicians, Nixon could never say this. Hoover maintained his directorship until the day he died.

The suspicious executive's tendency to diversify to avoid being dependent on a single segment of the market can also sometimes be a strength. Diversification may indeed cut risks and reduce vulnerability. It can add stability to earnings and provide many positive opportunities for growth. For example, in the beginning, Geneen's "conglomerization" of ITT made it one of the world's most powerful and successful companies, taking it from stagnant to profitable markets. It was only later that Geneen's "institutionalization of suspicion" made ITT insufficiently focused and less profitable since information was based on executives' insecurities, tended to become biased and inaccurate.[25]

## Weaknesses

The lack of a concerted and consistent management strategy is an important weakness in a suspicious organization. The reactive, piecemeal, and contradictory aspects of strategy thwart the emergence of distinctive competences and synergy among strategic elements. Paratech, for example, expended its energies continually analyzing the competition and attempting to safeguard its own ideas rather than concentrating on research and development, which would have helped it to get new products onto the market first.

For the employees, perhaps an even more important weakness of the suspicious organization is the atmosphere of distrust. The suspicious executive seems to be inclined toward furtive activity. Recall, for instance, the Hunts and their hired detectives and wiretapping, Harold Geneen's administrative spies, and J. Edgar Hoover's Clod Squad.

These executives seriously believed these means were proper avenues for organizational information-gathering. Such behavior on the part of the CEO will inevitably breed feelings of insecurity and disenchantment among second-tier managers and their subordinates, and a high staff turnover may result.

---

## Chapter Four

# The Detached Organization

## The Detached Executive

Lynn Townsend, former president and then chairman of the board at Chrysler from 1967 to 1975, radically changed his behavior over the course of his administration. A number of his top officers observed the symptoms with alarm.

"Something happened to [him] in the middle sixties," one Chrysler executive said. "He turned into a different guy. His outlook, his approach, his ability to take counsel and advice all changed. I don't know what brought it about, but things began to crack. He almost changed personalities."[1]

Townsend had come to the Chrysler presidency back in 1962 at age forty-two. At 6 foot 2, 195 pounds, he was a formidable presence as well as a financial wizard. In his first five years as president, he doubled Chrysler's U.S. market share and tripled its international one. He conceived the five-year, fifty-thousand-mile warranty and Chrysler's blue-and-white pentastar trademark. He had been on the cover of *Time* magazine during his reign, a young management superstar in an industry better known for cautious maturity and quiet convention.

"He seemed more like an old-style Hollywood film czar than a midwestern auto company chief," *Fortune* said in

55

1978, after he'd retired. "He was a handsome and dictatorial leader who enjoyed a high reputation as a numbers man." Even so, the magazine went on, "he never really seemed to understand the fundamental business of his company."[2]

Townsend achieved respectability for Chrysler through record sales and expansion of foreign markets, but such gains tended to be short-term and even more shortsighted. According to analysts at the time, Townsend's attitude had always been that auto manufacturers could gain giant profits simply by stepping up production, without regard to consumer taste. He demanded reports on Chrysler's retail deliveries every hour and pored over the huge charts in his "war room" at Chrysler headquarters in Highland Park, Michigan. Only a handful of personal advisors helped him make decisions. The 242,000 employees who worked at Chrysler—line workers, middle management, and most top executives—not to mention the car-buying public, had very little influence. Although actively involved in decision-making, Townsend had already withdrawn from people.

"Sales aren't just made, sales are pushed,"[3] he frequently declared. He was paying little attention to market trends and consumer tastes. Yet car buyers look for style as well as mechanical durability when they shop, and they weren't getting much style at all in a Chrysler. Although Townsend paid admirable attention to engineering, his management style so ignored fashion and taste that by the time he retired, fully half of the auto-buying public, according to surveys, never so much as considered purchasing a Chrysler.[4]

Townsend's continued withdrawal intensified the problem. He began paying less attention to the business at hand, focusing increasingly on outside activities such as fundraising for the Republican party and serving as chairman of the National Alliance of Businessmen. Visibly bored and distracted, he often approached project meetings with the careless, detached air of one who had better things to do, a marked change from his previous private, painstaking conferences in the "war room." He began drifting toward other careers and had, in fact, mentioned to more than one colleague that he was considering a run for the U.S. Senate.[5]

In 1972, Townsend's behavior became more extreme. His cavalier attitude had evolved into an apparent unpleasantness: he would call the ideas of his executives "stupid," even in public, and ordered division presidents around peremptorily. According to colleagues he drank more frequently, too, the martinis often making him depressed, spiteful, and indiscreet. At a new-model preview in Missouri in 1972 he recounted his troubles to an incredulous group of reporters. While public relations man Dick Muller looked on, helpless and aghast, Townsend told the press all about Chrysler's confidential problems and his personal anxieties.[6]

When asked in those days what was happening to him, Townsend was vague. "I changed because my job changed," he replied mysteriously, as if the simple elevation to chairman of the board could account for his strange new ways. One day, though, he admitted to a more credible explanation. "Once you're chief executive officer of a company the size of Chrysler," he said, "you've had the course."[7] To put it simply: The job had lost its charm and excitement.

The story of Lynn Townsend illustrates the characteristics that we have labeled "detached." The detached executive tends to be aloof and distant. This may always have been the case or, as with Townsend, may have come about gradually, as the executive loses interest in the day-to-day affairs of the business. Sometimes specific incidents are to blame—a divorce, a death in the family, or some other calamity.

Unlike with Townsend, such behavior is occasionally due to a serious mental imbalance. In the latter case psychiatrists have identified two basic personality types that fix upon this serious form of social detachment: the avoidant and the schizoid. Avoidant personalities, like schizoids, have had disturbing experiences that led them to mistrust others and to avoid close relationships. Unlike true schizoids, however, they still desire close attachments and social acceptance. In contrast, true schizoids often have cognitive and emotional deficiencies that render them unconcerned about their social isolation.[8] Thus, true schizoidlike detachment is usually extreme and is very rarely seen among top managers.

Some detached CEOs, who are neither schizoid nor avoidant, fit into a third category. Such executives show an increasing loss of interest in their immediate business but, at the same time, a greater attention to other matters. For this group of executives the paradox is that they can behave in a very detached manner in their business transactions but appear very taken by, and involved in, their new interests. Whatever subgroup we are talking about, however, to the outsider the observable behavior patterns show many similarities.

### 1. *Withdrawal and noninvolvement.*

Townsend's routine decision-making behind closed doors, and his reliance on reports and numbers rather than social interaction, exemplify the beginning of this behavior pattern. His later distractions even from the private meetings and toward interests outside Chrysler's doors intensified his withdrawal. Such behavior can have grave effects on an organization.[9]

### 2. *Lack of interest in the present or future.*

During his gradual estrangement from Chrysler activities, Townsend frequently attended design meetings without first having read the briefing books.[10] "Eventually he seemed to have lost all enthusiasm for day-to-day details and for the company's future. Many detached executives react this way, seeing the present or future of the organization as no longer worth their trouble. They seem to be divorced from the activities around them.

### 3. *Indifference to either praise or criticism.*

Townsend had a big booming voice and an erratic personality. He could be "charming and he could be a bastard," a colleague said.[11] In this sense then he cannot be termed a "pure" detached personality, since a third feature found in many truly detached executives is a cold, bland, and emotionless demeanor and an inability to express pleasure or enthusiasm. Also, truly detached executives seem to care little for what others have to say about them, as they are usually too uninterested to so much as acknowledge others' comments, much less react to what they have to say.

## Safer to Remain Distant

Truly detached executives, so aloof when managing, also imagine that the outside world offers them little satisfaction. It is as if they believe that all interactions will eventually disappoint or harm, so it is safer to remain distant.

Perhaps the best-known executive who fits our definition of a truly detached executive was Howard Hughes, who, unlike Townsend, took the "isolationist" management style to its limits. In his combination office/living quarters in the Beverly Hills Hotel, he established a "germ-free zone," an area in the middle of his room consisting of a soft white leather chair and matching ottoman, one small end table, and a telephone, which he painstakingly cleaned regularly to free them of "contamination." In the latter part of his life, he refused to go outside even for important meetings and forbade even close friends to visit him.

Gradually Howard Hughes became so withdrawn that he made himself a virtual prisoner in his own corporate headquarters. He let his hair grow to his shoulders, and his uncut fingernails and toenails curled out, like bark on a dying tree. Near the end of his life, he often went for months at a time without bathing or even putting on clothes. He began urinating against his bathroom door, refusing to let anyone mop up the mess. Churning out hundreds of bizarre, incoherent memos in his final years, he ultimately cut off all direct contact with other people, banning all phone calls. Not even his wife, friends, and closest advisors could reach him.

Even before his behavior became truly psychotic he had by no means been a run-of-the-mill executive. Orphaned and left a millionaire at eighteen, he had made a name for himself as a flamboyant movie producer and the holder of many aviation records. His Spruce Goose, the world's largest flying boat and his rumoured design of Jane Russell's cantilevered bra added to his fame. But because of his increasing reclusiveness he became known as the spook of American capitalism.

An associate once remarked: "It would be difficult to find anywhere a man of such wealth in control of enterprises touching so closely the national interest who has left on [his] enterprises so few traces of himself."[12] This statement, made originally in the fifties, remains true today. Hughes died in total seclusion in 1976, suffering from a degree of medical neglect rare even among the underprivileged.

# The Structure of the Detached Organization

## Leadership Vacuum

The company led by the detached executive will suffer from an absence of leadership. Whether the chief executive daydreams about other areas of interest (like Townsend's Senate ambitions) or sees human contact as scary or painful, as Hughes apparently did, the executive isolates himself or herself. Decision-making gets shoved to one side and productive activity grinds to a halt.

In some detached firms, executives on the second tier of

authority will compensate for the leader's deficiencies with their own warmth and extroversion. If that is the case the company may continue to do well. All too often, however, these executives view the withdrawal of their boss as an opportunity to pursue personal ambitions. The resulting arena of greed and self-centeredness endangers organizational stability.

Sotheby's of London, the world's largest auction house, illustrates this potential instability. The late chairman Peter Wilson, often stated, "You could organize yourself out of existence."[13] His management philosophy was one of minimal organization. Rather than tightly controlling his operations, Wilson allowed Sotheby's art experts total autonomy, encouraging them to poke around in far-flung collections and decide on the spot, and, without reference to the head office, whether to accept a particular work of art for inclusion in Sotheby's auctions. He also delegated to his administrative staff the day-to-day running of Sotheby's and made his art experts administrators of their own departments, a role few of them were prepared to fill. Wilson then went off on his own, handling only those aspects of his directorship he enjoyed the most, such as conducting the actual auctions and consulting with prestigious art connoisseurs all over the world.

This unusual form of leadership caused both expense accounts and staff rolls at Sotheby's to soar. By the time Wilson left the company in 1979 after twenty-one years as top officer, the situation was serious. In the last years of his rule, pretax earnings had begun a major decline. Perhaps as a result of empire-building by second-tier managers, the number of employees had reached alarming proportions: 1,560, a figure 50 percent higher than just two years before, without commensurate growth in revenues.[14] Sotheby's was left struggling to meet its operating costs amid a world recession, increasing interest rates, and a depressed art market. Strong leadership was clearly needed.

Wilson's management style had permitted Sotheby's second-tier management to work for themselves, not for the firm. Its art experts quickly became known for cutting commissions and waiving transportation charges, both routine expenses for an art house's clientele. Wilson's saving grace had been his extraordinary vitality and personal knowledge of the art world, enabling him to acquire many sought-after art properties for Sotheby's auctions and thus maintain substantial revenues. But even these assets could not offset the consequences of Sotheby's organizational problems forever. After Wilson's departure, the problems he'd created would become serious. Wilson's attempt to run the company through his cousin from France became a miserable failure.[15]

In spite of his failings, Wilson brought knowledge and energy to Sotheby's auction business. Unfortunately, his handpicked successor, the Earl of Westmorland, seemed to bring very little expertise in art or business. On the staff of Sotheby's since 1965, Westmorland had not sought the top job and, according to *Fortune*, saw his role mainly as that of temporary custodian. He had no serious background in either business or art, but what he did have were solid connections to the English aristocracy. A friend of the Queen (Her Majesty's Master of the Horse), he was well known and liked by English aristocrats, among whom were many of Sotheby's suppliers and customers. His appointment offered the company a public image of established dignity and centuries-old respect. One Sotheby's director labeled him "the perfect frame for Wilson's picture" at a Sotheby's that appealed to a refined and traditional public.[16]

Under Westmorland's apparently genteel, low-key, almost absentee leadership, feuds developed and jealousies and executive resentment grew. Various upper-level managers began jockeying for advancement, competing so feverishly in fact that one Sotheby's director would later recall: "Marcus Linnell, the chief of experts, didn't get on with Graham Llewellyn, Sotheby's auctioneer, or Peregrine Pollen, its largest stockholder; Llewellyn didn't get on with Pollen; Pollen didn't get on with Peter Spira, the group finance director; Spira didn't get on with Llewellyn. I've never experienced anything like it."[17]

In 1982, a few months after Westmorland agreed to resign, the firm recorded its first operating deficit since World War II. The lack of leadership had clearly taken its toll. As an American executive said after his corporation changed its mind about purchasing Sotheby's in 1981, "It looked to us like a giant mess. Our instincts were that this thing was a zoo. They have no internal controls. It's all this upper-class-Englishmen stuff. They don't know how to run a business."[18] Perhaps more to the point, some of the principals didn't even want to. The consequences of such management chaos were predictable. In 1983, after a bitter takeover battle, the American financier Alfred Taubman received clearance from the British Monopolies and Merger Commission to take over Sotheby's. After that, things would never be the same. But the takeover may have been the catalyst to get Sotheby's over the slump. The figures showed that following auction seasons ended quite well for the company.[19]

## Without Visible Displays

We noted earlier that a characteristic of truly detached executives is that they often seem indifferent to praise, criticism, or the feelings of others. We suspect that such behavior may frequently be a defensive maneuver against being hurt. Detached executives who do not abdicate entirely will therefore make decisions with at most a very small and trusted inner clique. Even with this clique, however, they will frequently continue to function without any visible display of sensitivity or enthusiasm, making most decisions unilaterally.

## A Fragmented Structure

The structure of certain firms sometimes involves leadership vacuums that diffuse decision-making power throughout the tier of managers one level below the chief executive. Such organizational arrangements may result in a detached organization. Fragmentation into hotly contested power spots may further weaken the leadership at the top. Though sometimes a leader's withdrawal can actually improve a firm's functioning (see Chapter 8), more often the firm becomes a collection of independent fiefdoms, occasionally collaborating for the good of the company, but more often looking to protect their own interests. We offer here two examples: Berenschot, a leading management consulting firm in the Netherlands, and Société Générale, an aging Belgian holding company.

*Berenschot.* In 1938 a young Dutch engineer, B. Willem Berenschot, founded one of the first management consulting firms in Holland. By the time he died in 1964, Berenschot's organization employed hundreds of consultants, enjoyed over 30 percent of the Dutch consulting market, and operated branch offices in Belgium and the United States.

Berenschot himself had been a strong, take-charge personality who enthusiastically endorsed specialization. Thus the management structure at Berenschot evolved over the years into seventeen separate divisions, twelve of which handled trade matters for specific industries, and five more of which related to functional areas—strategy, marketing, quality control, industrial psychology, and management information systems.

The vacuum created by Berenschot's death left his executive board without strong replacement leadership. Even Piet Koppen, the board's chairman, retained only one vote out of six, not even a tiebreaker. "Just before his death, Mr. Berenschot asked me to become 'managerial coordinator' of the firm when he left," Koppen later explained. "I was rather surprised since I had never even been a consultant and I asked him where I would get my authority. He assumed it should come from a practice of common decision-making by the board members."

Koppen added, "I was a naval officer for several years, but I am not military-minded. In this firm one could no longer function as a strong disciplinarian anyway—there is too much independence to do so."[20]

Until 1971 the firm was quite successful. But then income began to fail due to strategic mistakes, such as overexpansion, excessive dependence on government contracts, and most specifically a failure to adapt to a changing environment. True collective leadership prevailed as no decisions were made until all board members were in agreement—a relatively rare occurrence. The firm seemed to be drifting without any clear strategy and was beset by an aimlessness that resulted from fragmentation plus a lack of leadership. The senior management at Berenschot at the time became increasingly aware of this problem and decided to have as their next chairman a more decisive individual who could set strategy for the entire firm.

**Société Générale.** Although a lack of leadership can be troublesome for a company like Berenschot, where, for the most part, the firm's managers have the company's best interests at heart, it became more serious at a company like Société Générale, where managers may be more interested in their personal agendas.

Société Générale de Belgique is an aging, closely controlled conglomerate rooted in Belgium's industrial revolution and colonial period, whose portfolio dwarfs the resources of the Belgian government itself. It controls major shares in such varied markets as steel, transportation, glass, real estate, insurance, mining, and electricity. Founded in 1882 by William I, monarch of the Netherlands, it was at one time so rich and powerful that it had been designated, *Fortune* reported in 1969, a sort of kingdom all of its own within the Belgian empire.[21] Until the 1960s, it reaped fantastic riches from Belgium's colonies, particularly in the Congo, where even now it retains an interest in almost every significant enterprise.

La Générale's structure historically had evolved as a fragmented one. Its management board comprised specific industry experts representing the conglomerate's many areas of involvement. This historical tradition of being made up of relatively independent units reinforced Société Général's board members' behavior as independent barons. They frequently refused to divert the assets of one enterprise to another, even if such assistance meant saving a promising but troubled division from ruin. Also, their power as board members ran unchecked, as they completely controlled voting at annual shareholder meetings and usually maintained very weak "governors" at the top as figurehead chief executives. True accountability by the directors was lacking, and no independent audits were allowed. No business plans or internal policy decisions were released to the press, and board members elected themselves to the governing body and doubled as their own subordinates, serving La Générale also as its divisional operating executives.

"This board of managers," one analyst commented, "acts as though they've been conferred the right to take communion without going to confession!" Said a U.S. financier: "The French call the arrangement *une participation croisée* [crossover participation]. I call it incest! It has the same effects, after all, on the body corporate."[22]

With such a fragmented management structure and such self-centered fragments, Société Générale was setting the stage for a kind of gradual organizational fratricide. Given the existence of such an organizational structure based on tradition we can ask ourselves if it would have been possible for any CEO to exert the kind of leadership needed to focus this organization. The structure being what it was, intense politicking was to be expected, with decisions being made according to power considerations and little else. As a consequence, few concerted actions could ever be taken, as the company's resources would tend to gravitate toward the insufficiently discussed venture of the most powerful directors and away from the promising projects of the more junior directors.

## Detached Culture

A few years ago we came across an interesting example of individual managers fighting for their personal gain. We were studying Cornish Corporation (name disguised), a manufacturer of ladies' apparel, run by Selma Gitnick. Gitnick had for many years been Cornish's adept chief executive. She had recently displayed some "detached" traits, however, after the unfortunate death of her oldest daughter.

Mrs. Gitnick, already a somewhat shy individual, had become a total recluse, rarely leaving her office and never permitting other managers to come in and meet with her. Communication with Gitnick had all but ceased, save for those few messages that were transmitted through memos. For a firm that required rapid adaptation to its industry's dynamic and uncertain fashion trends, this kind of a breakdown in communications had serious consequences.

The corporate culture that resulted at Cornish resembled a political battlefield. Gitnick retained the right to make all important final decisions herself, but she was impossible to reach and imprecise about allocating authority. Her second-tier managers found themselves forced to make many decisions they were not sure they had the proper authority to make. Two managers, in particular, suffered severely.

The feud began when marketing director Mike McDonough accused design coordinator Nancy Kelly of incompetence and vetoed all her decisions. Kelly replied acidly that

McDonough had neither the authority nor the know-how to so much as comment on her activities, much less control them. Each manager then wrote memos to Gitnick complaining about the other and asking for intervention. Gitnick vacillated, first backing one only to be quickly turned around to favor the other. Such inconsistent behavior, of course, changed nothing, and the bickering continued. During the subsequent serious delays in product design, Gitnick's competitors stole a significant share of her company's hard-earned market share. The situation quickly drove Cornish to the brink of bankruptcy.

Cornish Corporation, like Société Générale, illustrates the detached firm's "fight or flight" cultural makeup. Its members are quick to protect their own turf and to use the leadership vacuum to advance personal gain if the opportunity presents itself. We also found this kind of infighting at Sotheby's as second-tier managers began positioning themselves for advancement and personal gain. A few top officers at Sotheby's had shuffled in and out of as many as three new positions in two years during Westmorland's administration alone, all in a frenetic quest for the most favorable jobs. The company's financial troubles, following this chaotic period, seemed inevitable.

In the detached management style, the chief executive's distant attitude frustrates the "dependency needs" of his subordinates, who would normally rely on a leader's initiative. This creates an emotional vacuum among the second-tier managers that, along with the leadership vacuum, needs to be filled. Howard Hughes, for example, often let urgent appeals from Culver City, the headquarters of Hughes Aircraft, go unanswered to the great frustration of his four vice-presidents. Their pleas for reassurance, their desire for a clarification of their respective authority would go unheeded, leading to severe intracompany squabbles and jeopardizing deliveries to the air force.

## Conspiracy

When Howard Hughes cracked, his aides decided to play up to their boss's fantasies, letting him act out his psychosis in whatever way he desired. Those who joined in his fantasies—corporate executives, former truck drivers, chauffeurs, construction workers, salesmen—consequently became Hughes' only contacts as they began to handle his assets. Hughes rewarded them with large salaries, extravagant expense accounts, enviable fringe benefits and corporate power. Meanwhile, their benefactor maintained permanent residence at Bungalow Four of the Beverly Hills Hotel, which became his own personal asylum until the end of his life.

A detached executive's withdrawal can eventually go far enough to allow a conspiratorial free-for-all. The company's objectives run a low second to fulfilling the entirely personal ambitions and goals of the middle manager. This seems to be the sad story behind the Hughes empire.

## Strategy and the Detached Executive

Gerald Trautman at Greyhound acquired at least a dozen major subsidiary enterprises in his sixteen years as chief executive. Eventually, Greyhound Bus Lines also rented cars, leased computers, insured home mortgages, sold soap, and ran Armour and Company Meats. When Trautman relaxed his supervision of the various businesses the parent organization became a disintegrated agglomeration of diverse and unrelated affairs.

"If Greyhound needs anything, it's strategic direction," a senior officer confided. "It's got to decide which businesses it ought to grow and which to divest." Trautman's corporate biography stated that the company's acquisitions had been "plotted as scrupulously as a moon shot."[23] Many observers, however, have been hard-pressed to agree.

"There is not now, never has been, and won't be while Jerry Trautman is there, a strategic plan for the Greyhound Corporation," a former division chief said in 1980. "This company has grown only in reaction to events."[24]

The battlefield culture of the second tier, in combination with the leadership vacuum of the detached chief executive, usually leads to catastrophic strategic consequences. Detached leaders, for example, often vacillate between the proposals of one favored subordinate and those of another, in the process growing more and more noncommital. Decisions are delayed, crises ignored. As we saw in the case of Selma Gitnick, with no clear or integrated market strategy as a guide, an organization will flounder.

The forgers of strategy in many detached firms will be found in the shifting coalitions of careerist, second-level executives. As these managers attempt to influence their indecisive "leader" to support pet projects or growing personal empires, the detached firm moves in one direction for a while, then reverses itself whenever a new group of managers changes the leader's mind. Internal lobbying becomes more persuasive than threats or opportunities in the outside marketplace. The initiatives of one group of managers often neutralize or mitigate those of an opposing group, ushering in inconsistency, conservatism, aimlessness, and change that is piecemeal, insignificant, and, in most situations, far too late.

A business analyst once suggested, for example, that Société Générale might be better off if it sold every asset it had and simply invested the proceeds in government bonds. Why keep pretending, the analyst asked, that La Générale's fragmented, politicized management style could ever really improve matters? So many of the company's divisions had been losing money for such a long time that, in a more open structure, major shakeups might have occurred long before. Yet bold, imaginative strategies, the analyst continued, had by now become unthinkable for the archaic conglomerate.

"It is harsh but essentially correct," replied Max Nokin, governor of La Générale at the time, to the mortifying suggestion of corporate dissolution.[25] Personal prestige, he admitted, had in fact become so important to the firm's warring fiefdoms that it seemed unlikely the bickering and politicking would ever let up.

Financial losses, however, proved to be the impetus for organizational renewal at La Générale. In 1984, Belgium's oldest and largest holding company broke with tradition by bringing in new top management. The company also decided to divest itself of less important subsidiaries and concentrate on key sectors such as electronics, information technology, and telecommunications.[26]

# Strengths and Weaknesses of the Detached Organization

## Strength

A useful aspect of the detached organization is the active role played by second-tier managers. These managers share in strategy formulation, and the variety of points of view they express may contribute to effective decision-making. For several years after Willem Berenschot's death, for example, his firm functioned collectively and well. Individual managers took initiative, despite Piet Koppen's detached style. The system thus worked—temporarily at least.

## Weaknesses

The most obvious weakness in the makeup of the detached organization is its lack of leadership. The most extreme example of an executive neglecting his leadership role is probably Howard Hughes, with his total reclusiveness, but the other executives—Townsend in his later years, Trautman and his tiny inner clique—displayed this characteristic, too. The behavior of such detached leaders creates emotional and power vacuums that second-tier managers jockey to fill.

One symptom of a lack of leadership is inconsistent or vacillating strategy on the part of the CEO. If Gitnick had come out of her shell, for example, Cornish Corporation might have regained its profitability. Like most detached executives, however, she offered her company, and in particular the two warring managers, only ambiguity rather than consistent and integrated strategic direction.

When second-tier managers are jostling for power, issues tend to be decided more by political negotiation than by the facts, and this is another important weakness in the detached organization. The cultures of Sotheby's and Société Générale, for instance, both ignored outside market forces in favor of fulfilling personal ambitions. Both firms hungered for tighter financial controls and had a shared vision of unity, yet individual power blocs in each firm negated common objectives.

## Detachment as a Secondary Style

Sometimes a decidedly healthy and activist management style will focus so much on one area as to neglect another, producing a "partly detached" style. Beverly Sills, general director of the New York City Opera, has now turned the once-ailing opera company around. All but bankrupt when she took over in 1979, it is currently in the black and thriving. But her fund-raising efforts in the early eighties nearly did in her and her organization. Battling both an accumulated deficit of $6 million and a crippling strike, Sills pounded the pavement and exploited the phone lines tirelessly in 1983 in search of new funds.

But as funds began accumulating, artistic woes grew. In an interview with *Savvy* years later, Sills admitted that many problems had been a consequence of her frequent absences.

"I wasn't around; nobody was minding the store," she explained. "I was traveling 250,000 miles a year to raise money for the company. I'm not so conceited that I'd say everything would have been fine if I'd been here, but there's no way some things would have happened if I hadn't had to call in and make decisions from somewhere in Wisconsin."

Music critics began attacking the shaky, underproduced performances. The *Los Angeles Times,* in particular, allowed no mercy: City Opera, it said, was a theater company where "foolishness has become a way of life." Attendance plummeted to a nearly disastrous 72 percent.

Though Sills's manner resembles that of a more healthy, dramatic-style executive, neglect of this one area, the company's programs themselves—City Opera's most important assets—produced a detached element in her style that threatened to undo all the good she had done, nearly ringing down the curtain on her entire operation.[27]

## Chapter Five

# The Depressive
# Organization

**A**llis-Chalmers, an old conglomerate in a dilapidated area of Milwaukee, fashioned its economic base in the second half of the last century around capital-intensive products such as milling equipment, steam turbine engines, and electrical generators. For many decades, this combination was very successful.

But by the 1960s, the company had entered a depressive phase as the smokestack industries began to wane. In 1967, one of its executives summed up his view of possible strategies Allis-Chalmers could take, presenting what seems an archetypal depressive statement. His company, he said, could be likened to a big log floating down a stream. The stream was the economy, the executives in the company were like ants clinging to the log. There is not much anyone can do, then, but hang on tight and go wherever that stream—the economy, or "fate"—flows.[1]

## The Chicken or the Egg?

In the depressive firm, it is difficult at times to know which caused what. Did a detached executive (withdrawn, uncommunicative, without initiative) despair and create an atmosphere of helplessness and hopelessness? Or had such an atmosphere already developed in the firm, regardless of any one executive's actions, awakening otherwise dormant feelings of futility and depression? In other words, are the organization and the situation in the industry responsible for the state of mind of the senior executives or is it the other way around? There is no easy answer to this question. Whatever the cause, in the depressive firm, usually a fairly old company lulled to sleep by steady, if unremarkable, success, the atmosphere is one of fatalism. "It is hopeless," the depressive thinks, "to try to change the course of events; I just cannot do it, I am just not good or powerful enough."

Although we tend to believe that the depressive organization predates the depressive executive, it is frequently impossible to know for sure. However, since the effect of a depressive organization on any executive within its ranks can be so powerful, in this chapter we will discuss the organization before dealing with the leader's personality.

## The Depressive Organization

For the most part, depressive firms run themselves. Both timeworn and bureaucratic, their organizations are usually dominated by administrative procedures that have endured without question for many decades. Inevitably, depressive organizations lose sight of changing conditions and times, since they function according to inflexible, outdated programs.

Top executives and the tiers of managers just below them also become unable to effect change or show initiative. They share feelings of impotence and ineffectiveness. Because of their sense of powerlessness they often fail to believe that they have what it takes to revitalize their firms. The organization then drifts along without any sense of direction, floating down rivers of ritual and routine and ignoring divisional goals, company-wide objectives, and the human beings needed to formulate them.

United Airlines, for example, demonstrated throughout the sixties how substantial this kind of organizational problem can become. One major external cause of United's problems was that its profitable Hawaii run was opened to five competitors as a result of the 1969 transpacific route awards. This route had been bringing in as much as $14 million a year, but in 1971 an operating loss of $17 million was recorded.[2]

Other factors also contributed to the company's malaise. By 1970, United employed forty-seven thousand full-time workers, seven thousand in administration. It was a "mammoth system," commented *Fortune,* "and [with] so many employees had come the lethargy and bureaucracy of size." Decisions were strictly top-down, emanating from headquarters in Chicago and slotted through a very long, hierarchical chain of command. Employees at the bottom saw no reason to offer their supervisors suggestions. Even the most practical ideas for improving services or cutting costs were sure to be rejected without being given any real consideration. The company's atmosphere was one of hesitancy, caution, and defensiveness. One customer-service manager remembers, "The company was very centralized. It took so long to justify things that by the time you could get it justified you didn't need it anymore." Passengers began to notice a listlessness among the ground crew, passenger-service agents, and flight hostesses. In the summer of 1970, United's pilots, though highly paid, staged a slowdown. "Things were going to hell in a hurry," a senior pilot recalled.[3]

## No Communication from Within or Without

Depressive organizations rarely engage in the kind of information gathering necessary to understand their markets. In addition, internal communication channels break down because there are so many bureaucratic levels and depressed and cynical personalities. Decision-makers therefore fail to obtain information that will enable them to make adaptive decisions.

Uninformed decisions can take a substantial toll if continued for long. The Melville Shoe Company, for example, had been producing a popular line of inexpensive and durable men's and boys' shoes since 1922, retailing its products through its nationwide chain, Thom McAn. Its first twenty-five years marked a period of tremendous growth: 370 Thom McAn shops were operating by 1927, only five years after the company's birth. But after World War II consumer tastes changed drastically. Variety and style took on greater importance, with women becoming a major new market for low-cost shoes.

Melville, however, knew little about women's fashions, since it had been concentrating for so long on men's. Its factories supplied only practical, unfashionable styles, and its factory managers, by now masters of their manufacturing domains, reacted with repugnance to the notion of following trends.

It seemed that they considered "style" and "fashion" nonsense. It took an uphill battle to change these entrenched attitudes. Eventually, a new president, Frank Rooney, was able to revitalize Melville and counter the factory managers' reluctance to look past their age-old routines.[4]

# Characteristics of the Depressive Executive

In 1966, George Keck became chief executive of United Airlines. A longtime United engineer, he had proved especially valuable during a merger in 1961 with Capital Airlines and had been chiefly responsible for smoothing out key operational problems during the transition. But Keck, characterized as an aloof man by the press and others, exercised a super-cautious management style in an industry that was beginning to need more aggressive and personable leadership.

Unfortunately, Keck's management style did not change when he became chief executive. He kept himself isolated, moved slowly on decisions, and appeared uneasy around people. When one board member offered to introduce him to government contacts, according to *Fortune*, Keck "ignored the offer."

"I was no babe in the woods in Washington," he was reported to have said. "I knew Gleed [another board member] thought you could go in and charm someone. I just don't work that way."[5] The result was $17 million a year in losses on a run to Hawaii that had previously netted United $14 million in profits a year. Board members felt if Keck had lobbied the White House and the Civil Aeronautics Board (CAB), competing airlines might not have been allowed to dilute the market.

Depressive executives harbor a deep apprehension about change and its consequences, even to the point of dismissing the need for change. Perhaps because they are "in charge of" organizations that run themselves, otherwise dormant feelings of powerlessness may come to the fore. Keck's decision to carry on as if nothing needed to be done, or could be done, about the Hawaiian run demonstrated a lack of willingness to really jump in and fight for his airline. This characteristic is often the sort exhibited by the depressive executive. As Keck himself put it, "I just don't work that way."

In analyzing depressive executives, we have observed the following:

## 1. Lack of self-esteem or initiative

Truly depressive executives constantly tear themselves down, seeing their lives as inadequate and inferior. They lack self-assurance, and are often plagued by a sense of both helplessness and hopelessness. This leads to a lack of initiative and a refusal even to consider needed changes.

We saw in Chapter One how Joshua Gordon, president of the Derrigan Corporation, became more and more reclusive over the heartbreak of a son on drugs. Not knowing what to do about this tragedy, Gordon shut himself in his office more and more, worrying and feeling inadequate. His slow erosion of self-confidence over family troubles couldn't help but spill over into his work.

"If I can't even handle my own kids, how can I possibly direct 8,000 employees?" he lamented one night to his wife.

Production inefficiencies grew to critical proportions, with some production lines coming to a standstill altogether. Even Gordon's highest-ranking subordinates could not get in to see him. The decision-making apparatus at Derrigan soon broke down completely.

## 2. Fear of success; tolerance for mediocrity or failure

Depressive leaders may fear subsconsciously that success will make others envious and hostile. This fear sometimes prompts them to "snatch mediocrity from the jaws of victory." They shy away from forceful action, creating a leadership vacuum and, at times, an exceptionally high tolerance for ineptitude and failure.

Whether George Keck subconsciously feared success is impossible to know. But there did exist at United a growing uneasiness with his management approach. Many board members eventually admitted they had said nothing about their concerns for months, assuming United's executive committee would "keep matters in hand."

Keck's removal as president eventually came as a direct result of this gathering uneasiness and intolerance of what many board members considered an inadequate performance. In 1969, as the country's developing recession began to affect major airlines, Keck announced a schedule of cost-cutting that struck board members as far too mild, and he resisted the board's suggestions to cut expenditure further, despite growing expectations that the industrial slump was likely to worsen.

*Fortune* described the climactic episode in the Keck drama, a board meeting in which Keck defended his record this way: "The board listened; some fidgeted; [one member] looked so bored he was glassy-eyed. Keck had misjudged his directors."[6]

Within a week, the board had begun searching for Keck's replacement.

## 3. Depending on a "messiah"

Depressive leaders, because they feel their own inadequacies, often seek out someone to protect them and to make the key decisions. They begin to idealize others—consultants, bankers, and other executives—and to believe such "messiahs" can solve the company's problems. Often these beliefs are merely attempts to transfer responsibility to someone else and to avoid facing up to difficult situations.

We observed this trait in a firm we worked with in 1981. A regional manufacturer of electrical products, Calton (name disguised) staked much of its turnover on its hundreds of independent retail stores. In our first meeting, President Ken Johnson commented on the growth in sales and high profit margins, but we were struck by his passivity and evasiveness in answering our questions. Often Johnson seemed to be at a loss when asked for facts or prodded to articulate policies.

When examining the company's books, we discovered that Johnson had been greatly exaggerating Calton's success. Margins had been slipping, a situation worsened by an increase in the price of supplies.

In spite of the poor performance, Johnson considered Howard Russell, a consultant recommended to him by two of his bankers, to be the cornerstone in the company's decision-making. At board meetings, Russell handed out "action assignments" and led staff discussions on goal-setting. Johnson told us he considered Russell one of the most "perceptive and important people" he'd ever met.

"He's a great boon to this organization," Johnson stated. "He sets us on the right course. He knows exactly where we ought to be going and how to get us there. If Russell were ever to leave this organization, I have no idea what I'd do."

In fact, Russell had accomplished virtually nothing during his two-year tenure. When asked for his vision of where Calton should be heading, he backed off apologetically.

"No, I haven't got their strategy or future so well defined at all!" he admitted. "I appreciate Ken's faith in me, but he's the president of this company, after all, not me. Hell, I'm just trying to get his company moving a little, to prod the boys into action." He chuckled, adding, "And whenever I can, to set Ken straight!"

The search for messiahs may be a manifestation of a depressive's need to avoid reality.

## 4. The pursuit of punishment

Depressive leaders, often as a result of unpleasant past relationships, experience a sense of powerlessness. Anger about this may result in wariness toward others and guilt, for fear that their anger (fueled by their sense of helplessness) will get out of hand. Such people may eventually turn their hostility inward and blame themselves for all that went wrong in their lives. Thus psychic pain may serve a redemptive function: Defeat is perceived as a just reward for their angry feelings.

In one of our consultations, for example, the chairman of the board of a restaurant chain became more and more dispondent as members began questioning the chain's low profit margins in resort locations. After a particularly intense meeting the chairman suddenly burst out, "It's all my fault. I'm just not qualified to lead you. I've let you down."

The members of the board were surprised at the self-denigrating admission. Their chairman seemed upset beyond the magnitude of the problem. One of the company's directors, a trusted friend, suggested the chairman see a psychoanalyst.

Psychoanalysis made a difference, and revealed one very interesting background detail. In therapy he recalled how as a child his mother would displace her frustrations about her philandering husband onto her son, telling him over and over again that he wouldn't amount to anything. She aggravated the situation by making these statements while others were around. And her continuing harangues had had a dramatic psychological impact.

Although he had tried to prove his mother wrong, therapy revealed that the boy, now the company's chairman, had always subconsciously perceived himself as inadequate to influence his peers, feeling doomed to fail and be punished. We can theorize that the pain and failure represented "just punishment" in the grown man's mind for trying to stand out and taking charge. Thus, though he had done so, over the course of his business career he had never felt comfortable, and was always the first to bail out and blame himself, and his own inadequacies, for organizational catastrophes.

## Depressive Culture

Depressive companies produce cultures that reduce personal contributions to a minimum. The organization is seen to run itself. Employees simply absorb or disseminate routine data and avoid initiating anything, thus establishing a pervasive climate of passivity, negativity, and lethargy. Employees and executives at all levels may also emulate the top manager's depressive behavior and attitudes. Morale falters.

The organization's automated nature and a top executive's weak and apathetic personality may not be the only factors in generating a depressive culture. An external force, like a change in competitive position, the loss of a founder, or a company's takeover by a conglomerate, will do the same, causing even relatively healthy executives to lose all sense of balance, authority, or self-esteem.

At the Disney Corporation, for example, Walt Disney's death in 1966 caused a compulsive codification of the founder's viewpoints, tastes, and ideas. In the cultural arena, this compulsive idolizing also produced deep-seated indecisiveness, a crisis in managerial spirit that has taken almost twenty years for Disney's executives to shake off. Their founder's boundless inventiveness had seemed so invulnerable that they believed the appeal of Mickey, Donald, and Goofy would last forever.

Thus when the pillars of Disney's mighty magical kingdom began to totter, the keepers of the flame in southern California slipped quietly into a state of bewildered shock. They watched Disney's movie division, for decades an unshakable staple of wholesome family entertainment, lose ground to Lucas, Spielberg, Eastwood, and 007. Then Disneyland and Disneyworld had attendance problems as double-loop roller coasters and video arcades proved far more enthralling than slow, safe cruises down the Congo in "Adventureland" or a visit to Epcot center.

In 1983, however, Disney was hit by the roughest blow of all: cancellation by NBC of *The Wonderful World of Disney*, ending decades of the firm's wonderful world of profitable TV hours, in fact the longest-running TV program to date. For the first time in twenty-nine years, the Disney Corporation owned no major TV time on any network.[7]

"People here are dying for leadership," declared Disney's new CEO, Michael Eisner, hired in 1984 to recharge the empire. "And they're dying to get to work. If Walt Disney were still alive and products had continued to flow out of his mind, this company would have no problem."[8]

The vacuum left by Disney's death seemed to have created a sense of helplessness among his second-level managers. They may have found it impossible to believe they could improve on the ideas of the founder. Their resulting depressive culture had undermined the company's originality and stemmed the flow of their unique, once-profitable "products."

Another example of an external force creating a depressive culture is the corporate takeover. A scenario might run like this: A dominant company purchases a weaker one, then strips its managers of all prestige and authority, imposing its culture without respect for the acquired firm's uniqueness. The dominant company wants the acquired firm only to produce, leaving it very little decision power of its own. Often this engenders in the managers of the acquired firm a sense of powerlessness or a state of resentment and malaise. Key executives will leave. The acquired company stagnates and begins to decline. Only reinstating some autonomy will reverse the process.

One firm we worked with is especially notable. The departure of the entrepreneurial CEO of Waverly Inc., a successful sporting goods firm (name disguised) occurred after a corporate takeover. The conglomerate parent radically changed the style of management at Waverly. Detailed control procedures were introduced, though many were in fact irrelevant to the business. A new marketing strategy was imposed on the company, one that might have been appropriate for the parent firm but was totally out of place in the market served by the subsidiary. This lack of understanding on the part of the parent eventually stifled initiative and induced apathy among the managers at Waverly, who began to feel, correctly, that they had very little control over their firm. Many of the most capable among them eventually left to take up more challenging positions elsewhere. After a lengthy period of stagnation and financial loss, the parent sold Waverly.

No matter how they originate, depressive cultures will very frequently be populated by unmotivated, uninspired top executives and characterized by buck-passing, procrastination, and lack of meaningful interaction and communication. "Decidophobia"—fear of making decisions—permeates all levels of the company. Such behavior may be the logical outcome of having been stymied in whatever constructive action has been tried, or may be due to a gradual loss of touch with reality. When the firm runs into trouble neither the depressive chief executive nor the second-tier managers take any action to set things straight.

## Strategy and the Depressive Executive

The approach of Allis-Chalmers to strategy during its depressive phase in the 1960s is typical of what happens in depressive organizations. Recall the executive's image of his company as a log floating down a stream. More often than not, Allis-Chalmers' second-tier executives downplayed the importance of managerial decisions, attributing company gains or losses only to the vagaries of supply and demand. In formulating strategy, depressive executives focus their attention totally inward, neither gathering nor processing information about the external environment. A proactive stance is lacking. Most of the depressive's time, instead, is spent working out minor details and handling routine operating matters. Decision-making is avoided; decidophobia and procrastination become routine; few if any efforts to adapt or grow can be seen.

Depressive firms will almost always be found in stable environments, the only settings in which they can survive. Typically such firms have become very well established over the years and serve mature markets, with the same basic technology, customer preferences, and competitive patterns as when the firm began.

Trade agreements, restrictive trade practices, and substantial tariffs to limit foreign competition contribute to the character of depressive organizations, as we saw with United Airlines (CAB regulations) and as was probably true with Melville Shoe Company (shoe tariffs and trade agreements). Low levels of change and the frequent absence of serious competition make the administrative task fairly easy for the depressive company, as its narrow markets are almost never broadened or redefined.

Such stable conditions cause the depressive firm to ignore the process of adapting strategy to the environment. Thus when market factors do change, depressive companies will not immediately discern any major problems. When problems do finally result in significant losses, the sense of purposelessness and apathy can preclude decisive reappraisals and even action itself. Often, strategic issues are never explicitly considered and meaningful change does not occur.

The case of supermarket-giant A&P is illustrative. In 1974, during the firm's long ordeal of shrinking margins and plummeting market share, *The Wall Street Journal* commented: "A&P's troubled turnaround shows how an entrenched and inbred executive corps can be caught napping by fast-changing industry trends and outmaneuvered by competitors."[9] Moreover, its present management attempts, the *Journal* declared, were much "too little and too late." The *Journal* saw no likelihood that the venerable supermarket chain would ever regain its former dominance of the industry. It even quoted A&P's competitors, who labeled the company "a relatively minor adversary."

"In their heyday," the competitor explained, "we were constantly looking over our shoulder at what A&P did. Now they've lost their edge. A&P's management was born of the Depression. The problems that A&P have run deeper than a slogan or temporary price-cutting."[10] The competitor might also have added that such management problems can in fact only be resolved by a total revolution in management style. If this does not take place, an attitude of hopelessness will paralyze action.

# Strengths and Weaknesses of the Depressive Organization

## Strengths

As we have indicated, the companies most likely to become depressive are well-established firms that may indeed have been extremely successful in the past. United Airlines or Disney, for example, have considerable name recognition. If the depressive organization can only be infused with new life, its earlier reputation may well help speed its recovery, and may thus be considered a strength.

## Weaknesses

The tendency of depressive organizations to live in the past, when times were good for the firm, brings with it anachronistic strategies and organizational stagnation. Thus, A&P's strategy of maintaining stores suitable to past, not present, demand, left it with too few promising locations and too many bad ones. As its customers moved to the suburbs, it remained in decaying urban neighborhoods. Its passive attitude prevented it from even noticing the changes in its market.

Another result of such anachronistic behavior is the depressive organization's confinement to dying markets. As societal values changed, Disney's maintenance of the wholesome family entertainment approach made it too stodgy and dull for most moviegoers. The market for "good, clean fun" for the whole family dwindled, yet Disney continued to produce it. Also, refusing to change with the times can lead to poor product lines and a correspondingly weak competitive posture. The Melville Shoe Company, for example, lost ground after World War II because its pedestrian men-only styles no longer offered enough variety. Its factory managers refused to believe the signs of the times.

Lastly, apathy and inactivity of the CEO, whether it proceeds from or predates the depressive nature of the organization, can only add to the company's weaknesses. If the depressive manager simply refuses to take charge, very little can be done to stop the downward trend.

## Chapter Six

# The Compulsive Organization

## The Compulsive Executive

In 1980 *Fortune* called him one of the ten toughest bosses in America.[1] In his Harvard days, at a diminutive 5 foot 6 and 128 pounds, he was a quarterback and varsity wrestler. Some of his critics refer to him as "Idi." He is A. Robert Abboud, ex-chairman of First Chicago Corporation, "an incredible guy," agreed one former subordinate, "who gets things done." But an assistant vice-president with Citicorp, John R. Taylor, added, in an interview with *Business Week*, that Abboud also "likes to run everything and know what absolutely everyone is doing. That may be the way to run a branch, but not a big bank with young, thinking people."[2]

Compulsive, control-oriented executives typically believe that absolute control over their organizations is the only answer to solving major problems. Fear of losing control drives them to dominate all aspects of their enterprises, insisting that everyone submit to their way of doing things. Relationships become viewed in terms of dominance and submission.

Abboud, for example, successfully halted First Chicago's losses during his initial years at the bank's helm in the late seventies, but in the process his management style apparently caused 118 officers to hand in their resignations within eighteen months, leaving many key positions vacant and departments badly understaffed.

> "He doesn't have the physical stature or charisma of leadership, so he uses fear," explained one of the original 118 who left.
>
> "He gave me a dressing down that I hadn't gotten since being drafted," said another, adding, "and when he used language I wouldn't use on my worst enemy, I almost hit him."[3]
>
> "There can be only one ruler here," Abboud reportedly informed his executives from time to time. "And you're looking at him."

His every word, then, seemed to become law, and subordinates, unsure of their status, had to toe the line until Abboud had created enough havoc to risk getting axed himself.

## The Saga of Sewell Lee Avery

Two strapping soldiers, under the personal supervision of the United States attorney general, were needed to eject Sewell Lee Avery from his office. They picked him up, chair and all, and put him out into the street. Dumping him unceremoniously on the sidewalk, the soldiers, with Francis Biddle, FDR's attorney general, began walking away. Biddle then turned to glance one last time at the fuming Avery, at the time president of Montgomery Ward, one of the country's biggest department store chains, and watched him raise a fist high in the air, screaming the most vile insult he could imagine (it was 1944): "You New Dealer!"

Perhaps for the first time in his career, Avery began to

appreciate the consequences of insisting that everything be done his way. A top executive since the age of twenty-one, Avery had once enjoyed the title "greatest businessman of the generation." During the Depression, he molded a motley array of thirty small-time gypsum firms into U.S. Gypsum, a $60-million plaster company that by 1936 dominated the industry. Confident of his ability to build empires, Avery then turned his attention to Montgomery Ward, a failing mail-order house and retail chain that was losing $8.7 million a year while rival Sears and Roebuck earned $12 million. Within three years, Avery turned Montgomery Ward around, converting the loss into an annual $9-million profit.

Avery's early successes, like his later failures, seemed to stem from his apparent obsession with control. In revitalizing Montgomery Ward, he assumed both the presidency and the chairmanship of the board, taking total command. His fascination with detail led him to explore every corner of his organization. Following a ruthless, penny-pinching policy, Avery pared Ward's budgets to the bone and cut all dividends until the company could afford them. Ward's had been wavering throughout the twenties between mail-order sales and retail merchandising, but Avery shifted the company's market strategy toward retail. He merged the mail-order divisions into a tight unit and introduced higher-priced product lines. In characteristically blunt fashion, he explained: "We no longer depend on hicks and yokels. We now sell a lot more than overalls and manure-proof shoes."

Unfortunately Avery was convinced, as early as 1941, that a second Great Depression was imminent. He hoarded cash compulsively, almost turning Montgomery Ward into a bank with a department store front, at a time when Sears and other competing chains were entering periods of rapid expansion. Avery's fanatical frugality starved Montgomery Ward, curtailed its development adaptation, and ensured its decline. His unwillingness to spend money on expansion began to show after 1950 as both sales and profits shrank.

Avery also convinced himself that only a dictatorial administration could get results. He thus became overly involved in operations and intolerant of employee criticism. When in 1960 *Time* magazine printed his obituary, it opened with Avery's own words: "If anybody ventures to differ with me, I throw them out the window."

Back in 1944, however, before his excesses had caught up with him, Avery himself had been tossed out, on direct orders from President Roosevelt.[4] Avery's obsession with total control led him time and again to ignore War Labor Board directives to make peace with the Congress of Industrial Organizations (with whom he would ultimately be forced to sign a contract). Even when a United States marshal had ordered him to turn the company over to government authorities, Avery had brusquely shown him the door. Not even Biddle's soldiers could convince him to yield this iron control over Ward's.

## The Four Faces of Compulsion

There are four primary characteristics of the compulsive management style. They are:

1. A tendency to dominate the organization from top to bottom
2. Dogmatic, obstinate personality and lack of spontaneity
3. Perfectionism; obsession with detail, routine, order, ritual, efficiency—and a lockstep organization
4. Tunnel vision

### *Dominance and Submission*
Compulsive executives generally insist that others do things in a tightly prescribed way. From 1935 to 1959, "Captain Eddie" Rickenbacker exhibited this trait by completely dominating Eastern Airlines. Already a legend, Rickenbacker had been a World War I fighter pilot who became a war

hero by shooting down twenty-two German warplanes in dogfights over Europe. After the war he continued his swashbuckling lifestyle by racing automobiles.

At Eastern, he boldly forged new markets by extending the airline's traditional New York-to-Miami routes into Texas, Mexico, and Puerto Rico while he kept a tight rein on the company's board of directors and 17,500 employees. He ran everything himself, taking care of each detail, and his personal charisma usually prevented others from challenging or even questioniong him.[5]

### Dogmatism, Obstinancy, and Lack of Spontaneity

Avery's father once told him if he "didn't stop being so intent about things he'd be dead in a few years." On the surface, compulsive executives seem efficient, full of pep and drive, and hardworking. But in fact they often act in rigid, unimaginative, and redundant ways.

This was demonstrated, as we shall see, by the first Henry Ford and by Eddie Rickenbacker, who after initial success hung on slavishly to unsuitable strategies in the face of severe problems and indications that these were causing grave dangers to corporate survival.

### Perfectionism and Obsession with Detail

The perfectionist characteristics of compulsive executive often obscures their assessment of the "big picture"—overall market conditions and the effect these have on the product line. An old hand at Ward's, for example, claimed that when Avery first took over, "he turned the place inside out, even to the fixtures and decorations." Every little detail was scrutinized. However, such CEOs, often paralyzed by the fear that they may make a mistake, put off making important decisions.

A more recent case involved Elaine May, the Hollywood director. "It was difficult for me to get directing jobs because I seemed sort of 'crazy,' " she observed at an awards ceremony in New York in 1986. Her reputation as a "difficult perfectionist," to quote *New York* magazine, has dogged her throughout her twenty-year-plus career. Some projects under her tutelage have seemed headed for disaster from the outset. Take, for example the 1987 Columbia Pictures comedy, *Ishtar*, starring Dustin Hoffman and Warren Beatty.

*Ishtar* cost a whopping $53 million, high not just for a comedy but for any cinematic effort, and the figures were due largely to May's perfectionism. At the start of on-location production, she demanded that staffers locate high dunes as a background for the many desert scenes. When a magnificent, dune region was found (with hotel accommodations to boot, an amazing stroke of luck), May changed her mind. Perhaps a flat desert, she suggested, might be better. She directed production assistants to have the dunes they had so painstakingly sought out leveled off for an area of a square mile.

On another day, she shot one scene fifty times with three cameras rolling, never giving Hoffman or Beatty the slightest direction. Late in the afternoon, after they'd finished about take number forty on another scene, May said, "OK, let's do it again. We didn't quite get it."

"Elaine," Beatty replied, obviously annoyed and very weary, "we got it before lunch."[6]

### Tunnel Vision

Compulsive executives have a very restricted focus. Although they often achieve short-term results, as did Avery in his early years, their narrowness can hurt. In screaming "New Dealer!" at Attorney General Biddle, for example, Avery expressed his outrage at trends that he believed restricted his freedom to continue to pursue his old policies at Montgomery Ward. He failed to realize, however, that Roosevelt's measures, especially the new union laws, were here to stay and that unionism was a sign of changing times. As a result, he wound up actually losing control of his company. Later these same mistakes would make Montgomery Ward lag behind the competition so badly that it moved preciptiously close to bankruptcy.

## The Structure of the Compulsive Organization

The main characteristic of the compulsive organization is a rigid, detailed bureaucracy with all its attendant formal codes, elaborate internal information systems, and ritualized evaluation procedures. Rules, not people, command as company policies dictate dress codes, employee attitudes, and even minute procedures. Petty details are catalogued and standardized. The resulting bureaucracy, above all, worships thoroughness and exactness.

During a short time in its history Digital Equipment Corporation (DEC) illustrated a few features of the compulsive firm. When Ken Olsen founded DEC with a mere $70,000 investment, few foresaw that the new computer manufacturer would grow to a $4-billion enterprise so quickly. Much of the credit for that goes to Olsen himself, whose personal demands that DEC's products be "solidly built, like military hardware" virtually created the minicomputer industry. According to *Fortune* magazine Olsen submitted his machines to rugged, perhaps even excessive testing, refusing to release a product until he was totally convinced it would do exactly what DEC claimed.

"Our strategy is to serve industrial users," Olsen said, reasoning that high-technology buyers would remain loyal as long as the quality control of his products remained rigorous. Fancy marketing was out since Olsen strongly believed that his machines would sell on their merits alone.[7]

This formula of his original success had a darker side. According to a former marketing manager, DEC's products became "the most overengineered and undermarketed computers in the world."[8] And DEC's engineering department became so insulated from the marketplace that six of their last eight products have been almost two years late. "They have an incredible ability to screw up product schedules."[9]

## Lines of Authority

The compulsive organization favors hierarchies. Here a manager's status derives directly from his position. Since the compulsive chief executive prescribes exact responsibilities and hates surprises, the organizational chart is a most prized document. Structure, not the person within the structure, really matters.

Thus Lee Avery felt he could purge his executives frequently without a care for their talents, almost oblivious about their replacement. In 1945, for the second time in less than a decade, he purged his entire executive staff—the president and nine vice-presidents. Avery introduced eight new vice-presidents at the stockholders' meeting that year, saying, "These men appear to have the character and principle we need." He added, "Of course, I can't see into the future."[10]

Between 1939 and 1955 some forty vice-presidents and four presidents were to depart from the executive offices at Montgomery Ward. Compulsive organizations become subject to the "Neutron Bomb School of Management": Buildings, flowcharts, equipment, standardized forms, and red tape all remain unharmed, ready to be reused, but people—living, breathing entities—are obliterated.

Employees who step outside their lines of authority in this bureaucractic environment of the compulsive firm run the risk of immediate rebuke or dismissal. They seem to threaten the boss's total control. A classic case in point: The original Henry Ford always saw himself as the sole designer of his company's products. Vice-presidents and engineers worked for him, took orders from him, and implemented his ideas.

But beyond that executives were expected to remain in the background to await their boss's direction. Initiative and enthusiasm struck Henry Senior as threats to his control rather than as healthy signs.

One day in 1912, after returning from a trip overseas, Ford looked over a few changes his chief engineers had made to the Model T while he'd been away. Thus, George Brown, an engineer who was there, writes in his *Reminiscences:*

> Mr. Ford had his hands in his pockets and he walked around the car three or four times, looking very closely. Finally, he got to the left-handed side of that car and he takes his hands out, gets hold of the door and bang! He ripped the door right off! God! How the man done it, I don't know! He jumped in there and bang goes the other door. Bang goes the windshield. He jumps over the back seat and starts pounding on the top. He rips the top with the heel of his shoe. He wrecked the car as much as he could."[11]

That the Ford Motor Company was rapidly losing its market share at the time to upstart General Motors should come as no surprise.

## Bureaucratic Culture

A compulsive executive's personality and his bureaucratic organization both profoundly influence corporate culture. Indeed, the workers themselves begin to adopt bureaucratic characteristics.

Even the renowned Texas Instruments (TI) exhibited a few traits we associate with compulsive organizations. TI justly earned its reputation as an innovator when its workers began thinking of themselves as "shirt-sleeved pioneers"—explorers, innovators, conquerers of new regions. Not content merely to harvest existing high-tech markets, they continually forged ahead to uncover new ones. But this creative image hailed by many as TI's hallmark deserves closer scrutiny. TI's top officers, former president Fred Bucy and board chairman Mark Shepherd, appear to have been two control-oriented executives. They would reel off memos and dictums day and night, practically sleeping with employee performance charts and evaluation reports. They had also been known to punctuate points they wished to make by pounding their fists on tables during their meetings, kicking walls, and throwing large objects.

According to *Fortune:* "If Bucy or Shepherd don't like something," one employee explained, "they'll interrupt the presentation by saying 'That's bullshit!' 'If that's all you have to say, we don't want to hear it!' Another senior guy once walked out on my presentation because I had bad news! Sometimes meetings became unreal. We spend more time at TI saying what Fred and Mark want to hear than saying what we think."[12]

One former TI manager told *Fortune,* "The corporate fathers don't have confidence in their people."[13] He went on to say that top managers are very reluctant to delegate authority. Others have described them as meddlesome, hot-tempered, and unable to see the big picture.[14]

In such an organizational culture, spontaneity and initiative may wither and morale may decline. A tightly controlled corporate environment may become rigid and insular. Valuable insights from those closest to the front line—salespeople, lab technicians, middle managers—may never come to the attention of policymakers.

Asked once how he might put his vision across more effectively during conferences in Washington, Shepherd replied, "You just keep saying it over and over and over and over again."[15] Middle managers, however, would quietly wait until Bucy and Shepherd left the room, then hold their own meetings. They felt, it seems, that they could not carry out the demands of top management, or adhere to the unrealistic goals or product plans.

"By the time I left early this year," an ex-TIer told *Fortune* in 1982, "lower level managers had lost a great deal of authority. Much of their control had been shifted into the North building [TI's headquarters]. Proposed products were defined and redefined there ad infinitum. Eventually you were just given a product that was a square peg and told to fit it into the round hole of a market."[16]

Often, managers who move up through the ranks within bureaucratic, compulsive cultures lack creativity or individualism. Submissive workers who are willing to conform to rules and squeeze themselves into pigeonholes are the ones most likely to thrive.

## Excessive Control

Overcontrolling leadership is common in the compulsive culture. At any time the axe might fall, slicing away status or the job itself. A company's workers must fit and be guided by the bureaucracy or the leader's pronouncements—never the other way around. And if individuals do not fit in, if they fail to follow orders precisely, or if they merely disagree, they can be dismissed.

The compulsive Lee Avery so intimidated and dominated his subordinates that they never knew where they stood. Insecurity ran rampant at Ward's and initiative was extinguished. Avery fired many of his most able top executives, even though this jeopardized the entire organization.

Questions were raised at stockholders' meetings about the "resignations" that had begun occurring with alarming frequency. Avery's reply was pure haughtiness. "I can tell you this," he declared. "I have never lost anyone I wanted to keep."[17]

*Fortune* commented, "When an executive is in tune with Mr. Avery, such a relationship with a man of his endowments and charm can be a stimulating experience. But if there is an element of discord, the scrutiny is a harrowing thing. If the heat is on, it is like a slow turn on a skewer."[18] It is hardly surprising, then, that Ward's second-tier executives suffered from a kind of shell shock.

## After You've Gone . . .

The Walt Disney Corporation, also discussed in Chapter 5, affords an interesting glimpse of how a former leader, with help from the organization's bureaucracy, can have a dramatic effect on a corporation's culture. In this case, the influence extends decades after the leader's death. Until recently, it seems, the spirit of Walt Disney, who died in 1966, stalked the company's corridors. His picture adorned office walls and the entrances to Disneyland, and his name was invoked endlessly. "What would Walt have done?" was asked before making any significant decision.

"Walt said: 'Everyone's a kid at heart!' " remarked one high-level executive with a wink.

Said another: "Walt also said: 'All you have to do is let an adult find a way to become one.' "

Since the founder's death, a new, seemingly bureaucratic culture had grown up to supercede the original wonderful world of Disney. Here all the leader's ideas were codified into a sort of executive bible, which dictated the firm's direction to the $n$th degree. Yesterday's blueprint for success became the current obsession, as leaders increasingly lost touch with their markets. Perhaps as a consequence, the Disney empire began to falter, delivering unpopular offerings that steadily eroded profits. This led to disequilibrium. Recently a palace revolution has shaken up the empire and is breathing new life into the firm. Earnings have been climbing.[19]

Sometimes, however, an established formula remains extremely viable and should not be abandoned. In 1984, *Reader's Digest* underwent a power struggle over this very issue, which culminated in one change-oriented leader being ousted. Edward T. Thompson, appointed editor-in-chief in 1976, was forced to resign after intense criticism from the board and from stockholders that his editorial ideas had strayed too far from the original vision of the *Digest*'s founder, William Roy DeWitt Wallace. From the time he pasted up that first dummy issue in his basement apartment in Greenwich Village in 1922, Wallace had emphasized in *Reader's Digest* what he called "art of living" subjects, generally articles on good health, parental advice, optimistic trends, humor or inspiration, and true-life adventures. Wallace dominated the production of *Reader's Digest* every day until his death in 1981, insisting on a patriotic tone and on articles low in both controversy and complex analysis.[20]

When Thompson attempted to update the magazine to more modern attitudes, board members claimed he was infusing it with "negative" tones. He had assigned longtime *Digest* contributor Carl Rowan a cover story, "Mr. President, This Isn't Russia," which attacked President Reagan's review procedures of subordinates' memoirs as a form of censorship. This kind of new direction for *Reader's Digest*, coupled with low earnings during the same period of time, eroded Thompson's power base.

After a replacement had been selected for Thompson, Albert A. Cole, an eighty-nine-year-old trustee of the foundation that controls the magazine, announced, "What you will see in the future will be a magazine dramatically different from before and closer to what Mr. Wallace would have wanted." The publisher of *Reader's Digest*, George V. Grune, agreed: "We want to make sure the company is consistent with the policies DeWitt and Lila [DeWitt's deceased wife and co-founder] left us."[21]

The culture of the magazine's founder is once more intact. But *Reader's Digest* will be in an extremely vulnerable position unless it keeps close tabs on reader needs and avoids any mindless adherence to Wallace's "bible." It is the extent to which policies match the needs of the market, not the nature of the policies themselves, that determines success. From *Reader's Digest*'s recent adaptations it appears that they are heeding this warning.[22] This is too often forgotten in the truly compulsive organization.


## Strategy and the Compulsive Executive

Until 1955, when the Civil Aeronautics Board decided greater competition would increase the airline industry's service to the public, Captain Eddie Rickenbacker had, for all practical purposes, a monopoly on Eastern Airlines' targeted market area. All he really had to do to keep making money was to control his costs.

In this, however, Rickenbacker went overboard. He began chipping away at both petty items and essential needs, sticking to aging aircraft, cramming passengers five across at first-class prices, offering cookies instead of breakfast, and scheduling flights to suit the convenience of the company rather than the clientele. *Fortune* wrote that Rickenbacker had the "cautious soul of a greengrocer when it came to spending money."[23] His frugality became an industry legend.

Rickenbacker's tactics knew no bounds. Semiannually he convened meetings of hundreds of Eastern executives, demanding that each rise before the entire group and give an exhaustive accounting of his department or division's previous six months. If he approved of the manager's report, he might respond with a compliment. But he chastised those who seemed not to be adhering to his frugal directives. He once leaned into his private microphone, *Fortune* reported, and bellowed:

"For God's sake, don't go giving away things we haven't

got to give. Anybody can give away $1. The thing is to give away $1 and get back $1.10. Don't forget that. Your whole future is in this company. If it isn't, then get the hell out of here."[24]

Eastern's reputation plummeted in the early fifties. Flying Eastern soon became an almost dreaded event. The airline's personnel were known to be unfriendly, even surly; booking errors were frequent; an informal organization called WHEAL (We Hate Eastern Airlines) soon sprang up. Finally, two New York businessmen were told one morning that their reservations would not be honored (the airline had once again overbooked), so they stormed out onto the runway and stood beneath the airplane's propeller for a full hour, refusing to let the aircraft take off. At about that time, Eastern's fortunes began to take a dive.

Seizing an obvious opportunity, National Airlines, Eastern's chief competitor, made its move. Pretty girls were added to its flights as stewardesses (Rickenbacker insisted on using only stewards), full meals were now provided on meal-hour flights, wide-bodied airplanes seated passengers more comfortably, and convenient, easy-to-remember schedules more sensibly accommodated passengers' lifestyles. Then the CAB altered industry practices by expanding the number of airlines allowed to follow Eastern's previously exclusive routes. By the end of the fifties Rickenbacker, still slow to respond to or even to acknowledge the need for change, had run aground. Eastern began a decline that would last well into the next decade.

Strategy and structure in compulsive organizations depend almost totally on the decisions of the ruling executive or a tiny executive group. Thus shifts in the wind may often go undetected until adaptation to changes is long overdue. Overall market conditions are usually ignored.

This may have been part of the problem for Ken Olsen at DEC. In 1983, DEC's net earnings in the fiscal year ending in July dropped 32 percent, an unprecedented decline for the premier minicomputer maker. Worse, DEC's return on sales fell below 10 percent for the first time since the company went public in 1966, and first-quarter earnings fell from $1.02 to 28 cents a share.

Something, Olsen wasn't quite sure what, had gone terribly wrong. But he personally rushed to plug up the dike, reorganizing the company internally and reshuffling his staff. According to *Fortune,* this initially appeared only to aggravate the situation, creating much internal discord. The problem, it seemed, stemmed more from ignoring changes in the marketplace than from any organizational failing within DEC. The once secure minicomputer niche was being squeezed by increasingly powerful, inexpensive microcomputers and even smaller and cheaper mainframes. Suddenly DEC found itself in a crushing vise. Computer products above and below were steadily nudging its "solidly built" hardware out of the picture. Paying so much attention to the quality of his own products, but perhaps not enough to the emergence of new ideas of the competition, the brilliant Olsen had been taken by surprise. Perhaps his carefully crafted bureaucracy did not allow room for viewing the big picture, so there was no effective response to the rapidly changing market. One observer, Donald Brown of Shearson/American Express, commented in 1983 that if DEC was to maintain its growth, it needed not only to hold on to its old customers but to seek newer, nontechnical ones as well.[25]

Texas Instruments seems to have experienced related difficulties. In 1979, Bucy and Shepherd decided to expand TI's focus into more consumer markets by offering their own brand of digital watch. They seem to have assumed, however, that their standards in the microchip industry—products with high reliability and minimum prices—would be sufficient to ensure similar success in this new endeavor.

Bucy and Shepherd established precise, thorough design plans, exhaustive evaluation procedures, and incredibly detailed production schedules. Every move was calculated, exacting, and checked extensively.

They failed, however, to apply the same rigorous standards to market research, dismissing suggestions of those closest to the market that fashion and style might make a big difference to consumers.[26] A meticulous, complex structure and overemphasis on design may have precluded a balanced strategy that adequately considered customer needs and competitive factors.

"Fred and Mark kept pushing to slash the price to $9.95," recalls a former member of the watch effort. "But that meant having a plastic case and band. We kept telling them consumers didn't want that, but they [Fred and Mark] wouldn't listen."[27] The watches didn't sell.

Ironically, some compulsiveness may be necessary in many turnaround situations, where tight control, authoritarianism, and extreme intervention in the details of management are required. In defense of Robert Abboud, for example, it may be said that though his reported detail-orientation, volatile temper, and insatiable need to dominate may have driven many able executives away, many banking analysts believed such rough, dictatorial management was just what First Chicago needed at the time to put its ledgers and consumer accounts into better shape. But when such a strategy succeeds, the executives who pursue it may become lionized, powerful, and doubly convinced of the inviolability of their policies and wisdom. The compulsive organization is often the result.

Even if their actions have damaged the company, executives in compulsive firms may refuse to admit it. "It took twenty-five years to build Eastern," Captain Eddie Rickenbacker remarked after his retirement, "and only three and a half years to tear it apart."[28] He seemed compelled to blame his successors, denying the consequences of his own actions.

In the case of DEC, an executive wizard like Ken Olsen has still come out on top with his own beloved arduous testing procedures. Perhaps the earnings decline encouraged him to reorient the company and pursue new high-growth fields. And DEC's renewed attention to the market is paying off, as its 1986 earnings amply demonstrate.[29]

DEC had the ability to adapt. Others take much longer to adjust. Such inaction can have serious adverse effects, as we have seen with Rickenbacker's Eastern Airlines, Avery's Montgomery Ward, or the watch division at Texas Instruments. It is ironic that long-term success can lead to over-confidence in an old strategy, deification of the leader, unresponsiveness to markets, and ultimate failure.

## Strengths and Weaknesses of the Compulsive Organization

### Strengths

The emphasis in the compulsive organization on fine internal controls and efficient operations can, because of its effect on product quality, be seen as a strength. Olsen's exhaustive testing, for example, certainly ensures that DEC's computers are as excellent and solidly built as he likes to claim. Moreover, compulsive organizations tend to have a tightly focused product-market strategy. De Witt Wallace always insisted that millions of American readers desire short, easy-to-read magazine pieces with a largely uncomplicated, positive editorial tone. When his successor tried to deviate from this strategy, spreading the magazine's target area out toward a more diffused readership, *Reader's Digest* encountered the only problem period in its sixty-three-year history.

## Weaknesses

One aspect of some compulsive organizations—attachment to tradition—may be so strong that strategy and structure become harmfully anachronistic. E. Cardon Walker and Ronald Miller—the two successors to Walt Disney until they were replaced—tenaciously held on to Walt's philosophy of wholesome family entertainment in spite of changing consumer tastes. Adherence to Disney traditions seemed to replace or at least overshadow careful scanning of the business environment.

Another weakness of the compulsive company is that it is so programmed and regimented that bureaucratic dysfunctions, inflexibility, and inappropriate responses become common. Henry Ford's refusal to alter even the color of his Model Ts, let alone make more substantive changes, derived from that product's enormous popularity over many years. Ford became reluctant to tamper even slightly with a formula that had proven so successful. Thus he ignored evolving changes in consumer tastes and stuck to his original, and eventually outmoded, design.

Such programming and regimentation take their toll among the managers, too, since they tend to stifle creativity and remove influence from second-tier individuals. Lee Avery's purges, Henry Ford's inflexibility, and Bucy and Shepherd's reported lack of empathy and meddlesomeness all seemed to result in cultures with low worker morale and initiative.

The five organizational types are summarized on Table 1.

### Table 1: The Characteristics of "Neurotic" Organizations

| Type | Organization | Executive |
|------|-------------|-----------|
| Dramatic | Too primitive for its many products and broad market; overcentralization obstructs the development of effective information systems; second-tier executives retain too little influence in policy-making | Needs attention, excitement, activity, and stimulation; feels a sense of entitlement; has a tendency toward extremes |
| Suspicious | Elaborate information-processing; abundant analysis of external trends; centralization of power | Vigilantly prepared to counter any and all attacks and personal threats; hypersensitive; cold and lacks emotional expression; suspicious, distrustful, and insists on loyalty; overinvolved in rules and details to secure complete control; craves information; sometimes vindictive |
| Detached | Internal focus, insufficient scanning of external environment, self-imposed barriers to free flow of information | Withdrawn and not involved; lacks interest in present or future; sometimes indifferent to praise or criticism |
| Depressive | Ritualistic; bureaucratic; inflexible; hierarchical; poor internal communications; resistant to change; impersonal | Lacks self-confidence, self-esteem, or initiative; fears success and tolerates mediocrity or failure; depends on messiahs |
| Compulsive | Rigid formal codes; elaborate information systems; ritualized evaluation procedures; thoroughness, exactness; a hierarchy in which individual managers' status derives directly from specific positions | Tends to dominate organization from top to bottom; insists that others conform to tightly prescribed procedures and rules; dogmatic or obstinate personality; perfectionist or is obsessed with detail, routine, rituals, efficiency, and lockstep organization |

110

| Culture | Strategy | Guiding theme |
|---|---|---|
| Dependency needs of subordinates complement "strong leader" tendencies of chief executive; leader is idealized by "mirroring" subordinates; leader is catalyst for subordinates' initiative and morale | Hyperactive, impulsive, venturesome, dangerously uninhibited; executive prerogative to initiate bold ventures; diversifications and growth rarely consistent or integrated; action for action's sake; nonparticipative decision-making | Grandiosity: "I want to get attention from and impress the people who count in my life" |
| "Fight-or-flight" culture, including dependency, fear of attack, emphasis on the power of information, intimidation, uniformity, lack of trust | Reactive, conservative; overly analytical; diversified; secretive | "Some menacing force is out to get me; I had better be on my guard. I cannot really trust anybody" |
| Lack of warmth or emotions; conflicts, jockeying for power; insecurity | Vacillating, indecisive, inconsistent; the product or narrow, parochial perspectives | "Reality does not offer satisfaction; interactions with others will fail; it is safer to remain distant" |
| Lack of initiative; passivity; negativity; lack of motivation; ignorance of markets; leadership vacuum | "Decidiphobia"; attention focused inward; lack of vigilance over changing market conditions; drifting with no sense of direction; confinement to antiquated "mature" markets | "It is hopeless to change the course of events; I am just not good enough" |
| Rigid, inward directed, insular; subordinates are submissive, uncreative, insecure | Tightly calculated and focused, exhaustive evaluation; slow, unadaptive; reliance on a narrow established theme; obsession with a single aspect of strategy, e.g., cost-cutting or quality, the exclusion of other factors | "I don't want to be at the mercy of events: I have to master and control all the things affecting me" |

## Chapter Seven

# Playing Organizational Detective

*The mere observing of a thing is no use whatsoever. Observing turns into beholding, beholding into thinking, thinking into establishing connections, so that one may say that every attentive glance we cast on the world is an act of theorizing.*
—*Goethe*

In one of the Sherlock Holmes detective stories, Dr. Watson decides to teach Holmes a lesson in humility by challenging the master sleuth to what he believes will prove an impossible task. Handing Holmes an expensive watch, Watson asks him for a reading of the character and habits of the late owner. After carefully examining the watch, Holmes comments that it has recently been cleaned, robbing him of many possible clues. At this, Watson seems pleased, since at long last he has put Holmes at a loss, believing the detective will almost certainly decline the challenge.

Holmes, however, is by no means finished. Taking note of the initials on the back of the watch, he remarks that it must have belonged to Watson's eldest brother, a not very profound insight since an oldest son in those days usually inherited such jewelry. Holmes then completely astonishes Watson by stating:

[Your brother] was a man of untidy habits—very untidy and careless. He was left with good prospects, but he threw away his chances, lived for some time in poverty with occasional short intervals of prosperity, and finally, taking to drink, he died. That is all I can gather.

Watson then tells us:

I sprang from my chair and limped impatiently about the room with considerable bitterness in my heart. "This is unworthy of you, Holmes", I said. "I could not have believed that you would have descended to this. You have made inquiries into the history of my unhappy brother, and you now pretend to deduce this knowledge in some fanciful way. You cannot expect me to believe that you have read all this from his old watch! It is unkind, and, to speak plainly, has a touch of charlatanism in it."

"My dear doctor," said Holmes kindly, "pray accept my apologies. Viewing the matter as an abstract problem, I had forgotten how personal and painful a thing it might be to you. I assure you, however, that I never even knew that you had a brother until you handed me the watch."

"Then how in the name of all that is wonderful did you get those facts? They are absolutely correct in every particular."

"Ah, that is good luck. I could only say what was the balance of probability. I did not at all expect to be so accurate."

"But it was not mere guesswork?"

"No, no, I never guess. It is a shocking habit—destructive to the logical faculty. What seems strange to you is only so because you do not follow my train of thought or observe the small facts upon which large inferences may depend. For example, I began by stating that your brother was careless. When you observe the lower part of that watch case, you notice that it is not only dented in two places, but it is cut and marked all over from the habit of keeping other hard objects, such as coins or keys, in the same pocket. Surely, it is no great feat to assume that a man who treats a fifty-guinea watch so cavalierly must be a careless man. Neither is it a very far-fetched inference that a man who inherits one article of such value is pretty well provided for in other respects."

I nodded, to show that I followed his reasoning.

"It is very customary for pawnbrokers in England, when they take a watch, to scratch the number of the ticket with a pinpoint upon the inside of the case. It is more handy than a label, as there is no risk of the number being lost or transposed. There are no less than four such numbers visible to my lens on the inside of this case. Inference, that your brother was often at low water. Secondary inference, that he had occasional bursts of prosperity, or he could not have redeemed the pledge. Finally, I ask you to look at the inner plate, which contains the keyhole. Look at the thousands of scratches all around the hole marks where the key has slipped. What sober man's key could have scored those grooves? But you will never see a drunkard's watch without them. He winds it at night, and he leaves these traces of his unsteady hand. Where is the mystery in all this?"[1]

# Making Sense of
# Neurotic Organizations

To some extent, we are all akin to Sherlock Holmes, detectives trying to understand and interpret the world around us. Of course, this does not mean that we always need the hard evidence of a drunkard's watch to help us make sense of the mystery. We are bombarded every day with data of all kinds: Some we instantly understand, some we spend long hours puzzling over, the rest we may not even recognize as relevant. But in every situation, our task is to make sense of things—to get beneath the surface, to disclose the undisclosed. Like Sherlock Holmes we are translators of signs: We must explain the import of the various clues continually crossing our paths.

If we wish to make sense out of what we see in "neurotic" organizations, we must pay close attention to organizational scenarios. And we must interpret the way these scenarios, or stories, unfold. Managers must take fragments or organizational clues and mold them into coherent wholes. They must locate hidden meanings, covert intentions, and buried motives.

In our consultations with managers and their organizations, we have analyzed company strategies, reports, statements, memos, and observed interpersonal behavior, all in an effort to make sense of the organizational scenarios that confront us. As interpreters we must stay alert to themes. We ask, "What is the true meaning behind a senior executive's metaphors? The motive behind a sales manager's choice of words? The implication of specific company reports, customs, or decisions? Do they suggest a particular theme or pathology?"

In short, in studying an organization, we search out hidden messages in the myriad "statements" made by individuals, groups, and organizations, probing into the perceptions attitudes, or wishes implicit in these messages. To understand behavior in organizations, we must get deeply involved, like Holmes, in the interpretation of signs. We are like archaeologists, decoding structures in order to unearth their meanings. Using "fragments" from the past, we stumble upon unconscious ideas and lay bare fantasies disguised but active behind such "facades."[2]

Our problem is knowing exactly what to watch out for, how to separate the crucial from the insignificant. We try to move backward in time to locate key turning points and initiating events that disclose the roots of a problem. We attempt to make order out of chaos, analyzing symptoms and classifying thematically related acts, statements, and decisions that suggest certain common patterns of sickness or health.

In this chapter, we offer you a disguised organizational scenario along with our own interpretation of it and some notions of what is to be done. A checklist at the end of the chapter allows you, the reader, to understand the reasoning behind our interpretations.

## A Case Study: Garber and Stone, Inc.

A useful way to play organizational detective is to look at an organization through the eyes of a newcomer. The exact role of the newcomer, whether newly hired executive, consultant, supplier, banker, or even a customer, involves interpretation and making sense of a seemingly unstructured situation. Newcomers will always tend to seek some thematic unity to help understand an organization.

But what to watch for?

And how to interpret specific incidents? How can a newcomer weave disparate elements and events into one integrated, understandable tapestry?

In the following case study look for the themes of this disguised corporation and determine how closely, if at all, the corporation reflects the organizational styles previously discussed. Note that our case study, in fact, is presented in a somewhat fragmented way. We do this to simulate the unstructured order confronting a newcomer or consultant, as he goes about accumulating clues.

### Frustrations at Garber and Stone, Inc.

Striding out of the executive conference room at Garber and Stone, a manufacturer, wholesaler, and retailer of high-priced men's shoes, John Swan sighed audibly, unable any longer to contain his frustration. For some time, Swan, vice-president of wholesale sales, had been growing more and more upset at the lack of direction in his firm and the confused allocation of responsibility among officers and senior executives.

The sales force of Garber and Stone, for example, operated like independent contractors, and the vice-president for marketing, to whom Swan reported, always seemed surprisingly indifferent—but not entirely oblivious—to the industry market trends reported by Swan.

"We have no integrated system for reporting to the controller's office," Swan declared at the executive meeting. "No way for management to connect with our warehouses. We've got to move on this and formulate a workable policy." Yet the others on the executive committee acted bored while Swan was raising the issue. His remarks were duly noted by the recording secretary for the meeting's minutes, then shelved for consideration at a later date. This was the third time this had taken place.

As Swan tramped down the hall toward his office, he recalled the afternoon in the spring of 1985 when he had been hired. Ed Rader, the senior vice-president of marketing, had taken him around Garber and Stone's manufacturing plant, the source of the company's reputation for high quality. Spiraling costs in the domestic shoe industry and shifts in consumer preferences to cheaper, modern styles, had forced the company to begin importing. Since the death of its two founders, the company had always been managed by members of the Garber family. Though the company had gone public in 1972, the Garbers still held 24 percent of the stock, more than enough for effective control.

George Garber, president of the company and grandson of founder Titus Garber, had held the top job for seven years now. His grandmother, Felicia, Titus's widow, had dominated the company for decades until son Neville (George's father) took over on his own. Neville served as company president for thirty-five years after Felicia's death, until he himself died in 1978.

Today, in 1987, many longtime employees still remembered Neville as the boss who knew everyone on a first-name basis, "the employees' boss," who kept a watchful eye on all company operations, personifying the firm's reputation for quality service. Legend had it that Neville Garber could stride into the workshop area, spot the one pair of poorly made shoes sitting on one of the workbenches, and know immediately who was responsible.

A highly successful cosmetics salesman in Philadelphia, Swan originally felt that Garber and Stone offered a welcome career challenge. "It could expand my managerial abilities," he told his wife the day Rader called him, "and really put my sales know-how to the test." After that one telephone conversation with Ed Rader, in fact, Swan visited the home office for an interview, with Rader and Jeremy Maxwell, the company's consultant.

At the time of his interview, however, Swan thought it strange, that his request to meet other company officers was given short shrift by Rader. "The other officers aren't available right now," Rader said, a bit uneasily. "Anyway, a discussion with them would not be terribly helpful." Swan got the feeling that Rader was antagonistic to some of his colleagues, but that he didn't want to elaborate about this. He also mentioned that Swan could meet Garber himself after he began work. Again, no explanation for such an unorthodox procedure was given.

Ed Rader explained the current setup of the company and its evolution from a manufacturer of quality shoes to a merchandiser of more fashionable retail and wholesale lines. Rader's hope had been that the decision to begin importing would restore profits to Garber and Stone. Between 1978, when George Garber became president, and 1982, net income after taxes had leveled off at around $400,000. In 1982 net income dropped, and in the following years the company sustained big losses while competitors thrived. Sales remained constant at about $18 million through 1986. But it was very likely that sales for 1987 would be at least 10 percent less than those of 1986.

When Rader called Swan to offer him the vice-presidency, he proposed a salary only approximating Swan's present income. But since the new job seemed to present exactly the kind of challenge Swan wanted, he accepted. In coordinating the efforts of the wholesale sales force, he would assist Ed Rader in strengthening product lines and developing new sales and promotion tools.

During their initial phone conversation, Rader told Swan, "The independent operator who purchases two hundred to four hundred pairs of our shoes a year is the backbone of our business." Salespeople were assigned to regions throughout the United States on a straight commission basis, although three salesmen were allowed a guaranteed salary draw that consistently exceeded their commissions.

In his first weeks at Garber and Stone, Swan saw clearly there was very little communication among Rader, Rona Post, vice-president of outlet stores, and President Garber. Swan noted that both Rader and Post had been hired during George Garber's tenure. (See the organization chart.)

One day, Swan had lunch with George Garber, and Garber recounted to him how he'd come to learn the shoe business. "I started out as my father's assistant," he explained. "Ooooh, I hated the place at first—the stench of the leather, the awful noise, the little tacks and the sputtering threading machines. But Father insisted, you know how it is, and so there I was and here I still am!"

Neville put young George to work at the stitching machines first and had him sweeping the workshop area and doing odd jobs—whatever needed to be done in the lower ranks of production. George said his rise was very slow. But instead of continuing with this history of his earlier days at Garber and Stone, Garber broke off this part of the conversation and switched the subject to an even earlier time—his stint as a flight instructor in the U.S. Air Force. "Things

ORGANIZATION CHART (SIMPLIFIED)

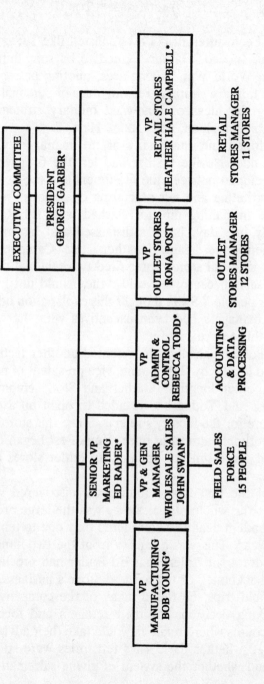

EXECUTIVE COMMITTEE

PRESIDENT
GEORGE GARBER*

VP
MANUFACTURING
BOB YOUNG*

SENIOR VP
MARKETING
ED RADER*

VP & GEN
MANAGER
WHOLESALE SALES
JOHN SWAN*

VP
ADMIN &
CONTROL
REBECCA TODD*

VP
OUTLET STORES
RONA POST*

VP
RETAIL STORES
HEATHER HALE CAMPBELL*

FIELD SALES
FORCE
15 PEOPLE

ACCOUNTING
& DATA
PROCESSING

OUTLET
STORES MANAGER
12 STORES

RETAIL
STORES MANAGER
11 STORES

*DESIGNATES MEMBERSHIP OF EXECUTIVE COMMITTEE

might've been different if I'd re-enlisted like I wanted to,"
he mused. Indeed, Garber seemed to be something of an
expert on World War I flying aces, quoting passages from
books on military strategy, relating tales of personal heroes,
discussing the ideas of renowned military strategists like
Clausewitz, Napoleon, and Liddell-Hart.

Swan found out that many of the managers who had
worked under Neville Garber had left the firm when fric-
tions developed between the old-timers and the newcomers
in the marketing and manufacturing operations. When the
wholesale marketing director clashed with Ed Rader too
vigorously one day, he was dismissed and his name was
never mentioned again. Heather Hale Campbell, vice-
president of retail stores, later fired two regional managers
of retail sales because, she said, "they could not get along
with their people." Swan thought this explanation odd: Both
regional managers had been executives with the company
for over thirteen years.

Rona Post, meanwhile, represented another faction, one
supported loyally by Bob Young, vice-president of manufacturing, another longtime Garber and Stone employee. In
1981, Post and Young had decided to open up a discount
outlet store for the factory's rejects. Since this store became
highly profitable almost at once, Rona Post began devoting
more and more time to opening up outlet stores in other
locations.

One of the first things John Swan discovered when he
took over the wholesale salesforce was the large proportion
of independent dealers who ordered only one to ten pairs of
shoes a year. This was a far cry from the two-hundred- to
four-hundred-pair orders that Ed Rader had proclaimed to
be the "backbone" of Garber and Stone's business. During
Swan's field trips, he found many of the company's salesmen making decisions for their retailers and focusing on
those accounts where retailers would take their advice. Swan
questioned whether these sales territories were still appropriate, and whether the system of giving salesmen straight

commissions on dollar sales actually had any effect in attracting new customers.

Swan was skeptical, too, about the effects of contract manufacturing on Garber and Stone's product-quality image. The main suppliers of fashion shoes were now a number of contract manufacturers, a major South Korean factory, and an Italian buying cartel. Product quality had become uneven and unpredictable, and delivery from Garber and Stone's suppliers was unsatisfactory. This combination of poor deliveries and rapid style changes led to inventory shortages, which inevitably hurt the company's reputation for customer service. Rader, however, evolved an elaborate justification for the status quo, cautioning Swan to refrain even from bringing these matters to the attention of the president or the other executives, let alone acting upon them.

Reporting procedures at Garber and Stone had become so haphazard that as time went on Swan began to feel thwarted in attempts to communicate his ideas. Rader, for example, seemed lukewarm about what Swan had to say about new styles, the success of new product lines, or the products of competitors. "One thing you should know about Rader's experience," confided an old-timer who was so prone to passing along company gossip and personal skeletons that workers in the shop genially referred to him as Deep Boot. "He hasn't any!" Deep Boot explained that instead of keeping abreast on changes in the marketplace, Rader relied entirely on intuition when selecting new product styles. "He won a ton of awards as a stylist back in the fifties," Deep Boot explained. "He was quite respected for his design ideas back then."

Swan also noted that if there was an important decision to be made, Rader tried to take it directly to George Garber, taking care not to let any of his colleagues surmise his intentions. Yet George Garber was rarely available. His isolated, ambiguous style stifled and devastated communication.

On the few occasions Swan did have contact with the

president—their one luncheon and two meetings of the executive committee—Garber appeared aloof and absent-minded. Once Swan sent a memo about a possible change in a major supplier, but Garber never answered it. Furthermore, Garber could rarely be found in his office. His associations with other executives were limited chiefly to his notorious "wandering lunches."

In the warehouse operations, Swan discovered a lack of any established reporting arrangement between management and employees. Once, flabbergasted, he watched Bob Young pick up the phone to call Arthur Koutsis, the warehouse supervisor and a member of the Teamsters, who was only in the next room. "The story goes they can't stand each other," whispered Deep Boot later in the day. Koutsis had had a hand in bringing the union back after the previous warehouse supervisor had been discharged. Though manufacturing offices and warehouse operations shared the same building, communication was now almost exclusively by memo or telephone.

Rebecca Todd, vice-president of administration, managed administration and control. With the company for only five years, Todd oversaw retail accounting, data processing, general accounting, credit and collection, and miscellaneous office systems. At executive meetings, she presented monthly profit-and-loss statements for every store.

In contrast to its retail stores, the company's discount outlet stores yielded significant profits. One day Swan asked Rader and Campbell how this might be affecting Garber and Stone's brand name. "I'm getting pretty skeptical about our retail policies," he remarked. "Emphasizing conservative men's shoes amid so many shelves of fashions for sportier young guys just doesn't seem the way to go today." He added that the practice of letting each manager have complete control over his store didn't seem to be working, either. "I've talked to them all in the past week," he explained, "and do you realize that none have ever even seen the monthly profit-and-loss statements which we compute for all our company's stores?"

"Well, don't hang that one on me!" Campbell exploded. Swan was astonished at Campbell's defensive outburst. "I won't take responsibility for that: It's those damned secrecy mongers!" Swan looked over at Campbell and then at Rader, who was keeping his mouth shut and looking at some papers on the conference table. To his surprise, Swan had uncovered a "bunker mentality" in the company's ranks—an entrenched reluctance to share information and arrive at coordinated, organizational action.

Each month, Garber and Stone's executive committee held its meeting, attended by Ed Rader, Rona Post, Heather Campbell, Rebecca Todd, Bob Young, John Swan, and occasionally by George Garber. During one meeting, Swan made a strong plea for the need for three or four new product lines every forty-five days. "The competition is clobbering us," he insisted. But to his amazement, Rona Post exclaimed, "I need three to four stores in that same period!" And Swan gradually observed that whenever an issue came to a vote, Post and Young nearly always voted against any proposal backed by Heather Campbell. The bunker mentality had crept in everywhere.

Ed Rader appeared less predictable. George Garber also wavered between the different factions, usually pleading for more time to consider an issue. Even when proponents of the various proposals made a sensible argument, the better the points made, the faster others would drive the issue to a vote so as to ensure its defeat. On the other hand, any poor, transparently political proposal tended to be discussed and deliberated ad nauseum, apparently to allow each vice-president a crack at scoring debating points, especially during the attendance of George Garber.

### Interpretation

Now let's see if we can isolate the characteristics of Garber and Stone and determine where it fits into our framework.

*Clue 1. The secretive and hurried hiring of John Swan.* This should have given Swan an indication of the fragmented and disorganized situation he was getting into. It was a first indication of the climate of suspicion and distrust at Garber and Stone.

*Clue 2. Strategy is insular, internally focused, and vacillates according to who gets the ear of leader Garber.* Only piecemeal changes occur and an overall strategic theme fails to emerge. Strategy resides in the parochial considerations of shifting coalitions of managers of discount outlet stores, retail stores, and wholesale sales, each trying to advance their pet projects. The interests of one group of managers, however salutary, are often neutralized or severely blunted by the others. Environmental scanning is totally absent here; the focus of the information system is exclusively internal. Losses, stagnating sales, changing market trends, and inroads by competitors are ignored or discounted.

*Clue 3. A number of uncooperative and independent fiefdoms exist in this company.* The sales force, for example, is highly independent and acts on its own over a very wide sales territory. There are minimal and unclear reporting relationships, and communication is absent between management and warehouse employees, discount outlet stores, retail stores and wholesale, and the stores and the controller's office.

*Clue 4. Personal ambitions and catering to the top manager's desires prevail among the second-tier executives.* Information is used as a power resource and therefore hoarded, rendering specific functionaries ignorant of crucial concerns. The store managers, for example, don't even know how well, or how poorly, they are doing.

### Conclusion

It must be quite clear to the reader by now that these symptoms of a fragmented culture, uncoordinated organization, lack of concerted strategy, and uncontrolled game playing among second-tier executives represent a classic detached organization. George Garber, the aloof, withdrawn leader, is the source of the problem. Garber displays indecisiveness and a lack of interest in company objectives and day-to-day affairs. His leadership style has created a company culture in which second-tier game players are allowed to run amok.

Had John Swan been more astute in interpreting this scenario at Garber and Stone, he would probably never have joined the firm. The company's current problems seem likely to continue unless ever-increasing losses, or some other sufficiently strong motivator, force George Garber to make a hard choice: either take a more active part in the company's decision-making process or, alternatively, withdraw completely and bring in a new CEO.

# Rules of Interpretation

Given the predicament in which John Swan found himself, it seems appropriate to propose a number of tentative rules for the interpretation of a management situation, keeping in mind that organizational "scripts" are written by an individual or group of individuals and can become codified over time. There are four principal features to keep in mind:

## Thematic Unity

When we observe an organizational scenario, we try to shape our different observations into one interconnected, cohesive unit. In Garber and Stone we looked for some sense of communality among the various themes. The interplay of the detached leadership style of Garber and the resulting detached organization and all its disjointed but interrelated parts became most central.

## Pattern Matching

In interpreting an organizational situation, we search for structural parallels. We hope to find a "fit" between present-day events and past incidents, primarily applicable to the CEO, but also concerning an organization's history. In short, we seek revealing repetition.

Pattern matching relates to the tendency in each of us to become entangled in memories of the past. Interpreting the present in terms of the past, we relive it and react as we did at a previous time. But what may have been a very appropriate reaction at one time now becomes ineffective and anachronistic.

Thus we observed that Garber and Stone's retail stores continued to stock conservatively styled shoes, harking back to a time when these had been the company's hallmark, rather than taking into account present market trends for more fashionable, flashier styles. Similarly, Rader still relied on his judgment of styles, which had proved successful two decades earlier, but now often represented poor style decisions for a very changed, volatile environment.

## Psychological Urgency

Somewhere in the scenario or "text" it is always possible to identify the most pressing problem. At Garber and Stone, the president's wish to withdraw and the power-hungry second-tier managers' narcissistic interests and lack of concern with what might be beneficial to the overall company seemed at the core of its difficulties.

## Multiple Function

An organizational scenario may have more than one meaning and can be looked at from many different points of view. Sometimes, defensive processes will stand out. Other times key dynamics may be more related to how aggression is managed, how executives deal with affectionate relationships, or how interpersonal behavior patterns affect the overall organization.

To complicate matters even further, these issues may all play a concurrent role and occur simultaneously at the individual, cultural and organizational levels. We observed all these dynamics to be at work at Garber and Stone.

Becoming familiar with these rules of interpretation and having some knowledge about basic themes and configurations can enable us to become true "pattern finders" and discover significance in things that at first glance might seem meaningless or chaotic. When we get right down to it, this is really what the task of a manager is all about. Effective managers are very skilled in the process we call sensemaking. And they are quick to identify key themes and select the most critical information needed for profitable decision making.

# Assessing Your Firm

You may wish to play detective with your own firm to determine whether it resembles any of our five dysfunctional types. Using the following checklist, answer yes or no to all questions in categories A to E. Then address the general thematic questions that conclude this section.

But a word of caution is in order before completing the

questionnaire. This questionnaire is designed to encourage you to think about organizational types. It does not have the scientific properties of a validated test.

## Category A

YES   NO

1. Is power within the organization highly centralized in the hands of the chief executive?

2. Is there a very strong organizational culture in which everyone at the managerial level sees things pretty much the same way?

3. Is the CEO put on a pedestal by many employees?

4. Is there suppression of dissent and contrary opinon by getting rid of "rebels" or ignoring them?

5. Does the CEO seem overburdened with work because he or she tries to do everything him or herself?

6. Are there many grandiose and risky ventures that jeopardize corporate solvency or deplete resources?

7. Does the CEO make decisions rapidly and without consultation?

8. Is the firm rapidly diversifying, introducing many new products, or expanding geographically in a way that taxes resources?

9. Does the CEO appear to be vain or egotistical?

10. Are sycophants and toadies the only ones rewarded with promotion?

11. Does most information flow down rather than up the hierarchy?

12. Does the strategy of the firm reside mainly in the mind of the CEO?

13. Are growth and expansion pursued seemingly for their own sake?

## Category B

1. Is there an atmosphere of suspicion and distrust in the firm?

2. Do managers identify and pay a great deal of attention to external "enemies," such as the government and competitors, blaming them for their failures or using them as the basis for formulating strategy?

3. Is there a strong emphasis on management information systems to identify managerial inadequacies and assign blame?

4. Are there corporate "spies" that inform top managers of goings-on down the line?

5. Is corporate loyalty a big factor in assessing an employee?

YES   NO

6. Does the CEO have a siege mentality? Does he or she constantly prefer to defend against or attack the competition?

7. Is the corporate strategy too much a reaction to what competitors are doing and not enough an attempt to build on unique competences?

8. Is there much secrecy regarding information on performance, salaries, decisions, etc.?

9. Does the firm's strategy vacillate too much according to external conditions?

10. Is there excessive risk avoidance?

11. Is the firm overly diversified?

## Category C

YES   NO

1. Is the firm badly split, with much disagreement among the various departments or divisions?

2. Does political infighting occur very often?

3. Is the CEO somewhat reclusive, refraining from personal contact and preferring to communicate by memo?

4. Is there a leadership vacuum?

5. Do decisions get delayed for long periods of time because of squabbling?

6. Do the personal ambitions of managers take dramatic precedence over overall organizational goals?

7. Are strategies badly fragmented, vacillating between one approach and another, according to which senior executive is favored by the CEO?

8. Is the top executive too busy with outside matters to pay much attention to the firm and its business?

9. Do very few decisions emanate from the top of the organization as things just drift along?

10. Is it difficult to perceive what the CEO really wants?

## Category D

YES   NO

1. Is there a feeling of helplessness to influence events on the part of the CEO or the key top managers?

2. Has the firm stagnated while competitors have advanced?

3. Are product lines and services antiquated?

4. Is there very little scanning of the environment?

5. Are production facilities poor and inefficient?

YES   NO

6. Are strategies very narrow and resistant to change?

7. Is there a lack of action, an atmosphere of decision paralysis?

8. Do many young, aggressive managers leave the organization because of the stifling climate and the lack of opportunity for advancement?

9. Is there extreme conservatism in capital expenditure?

10. Do bureaucratic rules set long ago replace communication and deliberation in decision-making?

## Category E

YES   NO

1. Is the firm very bureaucratic, filled with red tape, regulations, formal policies and procedures, and the like?

2. Is there a tendency for precedents to decide issues more than analysis or discussion?

3. Has strategy remained essentially the same for many years?

4. Is the firm slow to adapt to trends in the marketplace?

5. Does the CEO hoard power?

YES   NO

6. Is the CEO overly concerned with one or two elements of strategy, e.g., efficiency, productivity, or costs, to the exclusion of most others?

7. Did a founder or former CEO leave a strategic legacy that is held to be sacrosanct by current managers?

8. Are strategies very precisely articulated, down to the last detail?

9. Do information systems provide too much "hard" data on internal issues—costs, scrap rates—and too little "soft" data on market trends, customer reactions, etc?

10. Does the CEO prefer subordinates who follow his or her directives very precisely and refrain from arguing?

11. Is there a great emphasis on position and status?

## Interpreting the Checklist Responses

If you have responded in the affirmative to only two or three questions in each category, you are probably not working in one of our troubled organizations. If, however, you have answered yes to more than half the questions in a given category, you are most likely in an organization that resembles—at least to a degree—one or more of our neurotic types. Our categories are coded as follows:

A: Dramatic

B: Suspicious

C: Detached

D: Depressive

E: Compulsive

Organizations that fall into one or more of our five categories can be very unpleasant places to work and will be unlikely to change much from within without extreme pressure to do so.

You can also use the checklist to see which attributes you dislike most in each category. For each question, measure how irritating the attribute described is by assigning a score of 3 for Unbearable, 2 for Bothersome, or 1 for Acceptable. By adding up the scores in each category, you can determine the kind of organization you should most avoid.

To check further the correspondence of your own firm with those of the five types we discussed, the following general questions can be useful. These may reveal crucial themes that characterize various aspects of an organization. They show the culture, the inner workings of the organization—"what makes the firm tick"—and reveal whether there are further symptoms indicative of the five types.

## General Questions

1. What is the working environment like?

2. What does the organization stand for? What are its goals?

3. What are the "dreams" of the CEO?

4. What aspects of organizational functioning are important to the leaders? What gets them excited (angry, pleased)?

5. How are crisis and critical incidents dealt with?

6. What kind of people do well in the organization?

7. What are the measures of performance and the criteria for rewards and punishments?

8. What are the criteria for selection, promotion, and termination?

9. What kind of organizational "war stories" and rituals exist? What are the taboos?

10. What is the nature of the organization's structure?

A manager's central task is to discover underlying themes in the different managerial stories that describe his or her organization. We would like to repeat again that to do so, managers must be extremely attentive listeners and observers. They must pay close attention to the way in which stories are presented, and try to penetrate these texts and understand their full significance. To be a good organizational detective, a manager has to develop an acute sense of empathy, experiencing how the "narrator" of a story—often the company's CEO—reacts to the world at large to give it form and meaning. Recall the words of Louis Pasteur: "In the field of observation, chance favors only the prepared minds."

--- **Chapter Eight** ---

# Why Some Companies (and Their CEOs) Resist Change (and What to Do About It)

*The undiscovered country from whose bourn*
*No traveller returns, puzzles the will,*
*And makes us rather bear those ills we have*
*Than fly to others that we know not of.*
                                    *Hamlet*

**P**ain, the greatest stimulus for change we know, cannot help but command our attention. And when executives or organizations are required to change long-standing habits, oftentimes only pain will move them. It may take a health crisis—a medical emergency, perhaps, such as a coronary, to make a hard-driving executive slow down and take account of his life and career. Similarly, it may take a severe decline in performance to motivate organizational change.

Resistance to change, however, during threatening situations, is an ironic companion. So unless overwhelming forces, like some form of "pain," compel action, quite possibly not much will change.

For the neurotic organization, pain can arise in many forms: an exceptionally high rate of turnover or absenteeism; grave inefficiencies; labor problems, possibly a strike; changes in management; and, we have seen from many of our examples, falling sales and profits. And there are painful, external pressures, too: threats from competitors' marketing campaigns; or new products; scarcity of resources, such as raw materials or capital; the impact of technology; a changing/adverse government legislation; suppliers; and consumer groups.

The biggest problem with change, however, lies in its timing: Too often, because of management resistance, needed change comes about only after tremendous pressures have wrought critical damage. Sometimes, the organization never recovers.

Why do individuals and organizations resist change? One reason is that change tends to destroy social relationships and redistribute power. Secondly, change can lower a manager's status, alter his job or reduce his freedom.

Change may also be resisted when it is imposed peremptorily, without explanation or involvement by those affected. And it may even be resisted when viewed as too expensive—as in purchasing new equipment, perhaps, or relocating to a modern plant. Often forgotten are the tremendous costs of *not* changing and the insidious, debilitating effects of the status quo.

In this chapter, we explore obstacles—we call them "blockades"—to adaptation and change, especially as they apply to our five types of neurotic organizations. In surveying three categories of blockades—personal, cultural, and organizational—we define and illustrate their dynamics so that you may recognize them in your own organization. At the conclusion of this chapter, and in the final two chapters of the book, we suggest possible solutions to these problems and explore ideas for breaking down resistances to adaptation.

## Personal Blockades

Adapting to change requires strengths that overcome pain and bewilderment. The psychological makeup of a CEO may greatly influence his or her adaptive powers. Most important are the defensive reactions employed—the executive's self-image, manner of dealing with anxiety and depression, ability to learn and engage in constructive endeavors, and finally, an ability to measure wishes and hopes against what is realistically possible.

Different people have different ways of defending themselves against painful ideas or events. CEOs, when faced with problems in their companies, are no exception. A common defense mechanism we have seen is "splitting" —categorizing concepts and individuals as either wholly good or wholly bad. Recall suspicious executive Henry Ford I's deep distrust of unions. These new gatherings of workers were so "bad," he believed, that even inflicting violence upon them was justified.

In the other direction, we see unrestrained "idealization"— overestimation of others, a belief that someone or something can do no wrong. Thus, as in the case of Calton in the chapter on depressive executives, CEO Johnson managed to convince himself that his consultant could singlehandedly keep the company on the right course and had all the answers to the company's problems. In this way he defended himself against his own sense of helplessness. Moreover, he "denied" how desperate the situation really was in his company.

Alternatively, some CEOs attempt to project their own problems onto others. Henry Ford II, for example, was so upset and frustrated at the unexpected success of a subordinate, Lee Iacocca, that he sacked him, claiming he had been sneaking around behind his back. Lee Avery thought all his problems stemmed from FDR and his "New Dealers." J. Edgar Hoover simply blamed almost *everybody*.

We delineate three principal categories of "defenders" —how executives deal with stressful events: the Self-Doubting Thomas, the Emotional Defender, and the Hope Addict. Psychiatrists tell us the more one resorts to such defensive strategies, the more difficult adaptation will be. Moreover, the individual who excessively and rigidly uses a particular defense or group of defenses will find change more difficult than one who uses defenses more discriminatingly and flexibly.[1]

## The Self-Doubting Thomas

Lack of a positive and stable self-image is one barrier that may come between a leader and the forces of change. The self-doubter harbors feelings of estrangement, confusion, anxiety, and emptiness. "I am no good as I am now, I can do nothing right, I'm really a fake" goes the inner dialogue. In a given situation some people may even act as someone else they know would act, rather than in a way more genuinely their own. They acquire gestures, phrases, ideologies, and lifestyles from others.

Although a seemingly confident executive, John De Lorean made himself over completely, during an apparent mid-life crisis, taking a body type from athletes of the day and a social persona from Hollywood celebrities. Perhaps his dramatic transformation may be seen in the context of being dissatisfied with his self-image, the one acquired during his early years at General Motors.[2]

At United Airlines, too, CEO Keck's unwillingness to take forceful action may have stemmed from this feeling, common to all of us at certain moments, that to take an aggressive position might mean risking too much. Indeed, a strong sense of identity is needed to allow individuals to feel at ease with themselves and to have an integrated concept of self. This makes it possible to remain the same amid change, whether painful or otherwise.[3]

To avoid the Self-Doubting Thomas syndrome, an executive must succeed in balancing inner and outer worlds, a process that can be achieved only through continual self-examination, positive reinforcement, and renewal. Such adaptability will obviously be useful toward accepting the need for change in one's organization. But there are no easy ways to attain this.

## The Emotional Defender

CEOs may also react in different emotional ways to anxiety and depression. Dramatic executives, for example, react impulsively and arbitrarily to anxiety, abruptly relocating their companies or making acquisitions without careful consideration and planning. Unimportant issues may trigger displays of irrational anger. De Lorean, for example, erupted into fits of rage whenever a subordinate seemed to steal his media limelight. If an executive's tolerance of depression is low, this may also prove a blockade to change: Depressive executives sink into deep despair and are tougher to motivate than those buoyant enough to pick up the pieces and get started on something new.

In general, then, managers sufficiently able to remain in control when faced with great stress are far more receptive and adaptive to change than executives who succumb more easily to impulse or despair.[4] Some executives have found that psychotherapy, stress-management programs, or even one of the various forms of self-help available today have assisted their previously overreactive defenses in times of intense stress.[5]

## The Hope Addict

A CEO's realism and ability to balance wishes and hopes against what is truly possible also affects productive adaptability. But sometimes dreams far exceed reality—as in Ludwig's Brazilian scheme. Or CEOs refuse to acknowledge unpleasant information—as did Redfield at Itel. Here executives cling to what they would like to hear, not what is true, "hanging on hope," wishing for some messianic development to come along and save the day.

On the other hand, when executives constantly test their personal wishes against reality, they will be more truly creative, productive, and unscarred by "painful" change. And we have observed positive traits that can promote receptivity to change and render it less painful, including an ability to engage in constructive endeavors and to learn how to welcome even the worst news. Some organizations use various types of discussion groups to lay bare potential threats and foster a better understanding of unpleasant realities. They do this by examining possible solutions, balancing the negative with the positive.

# Cultural Blockades

*Culture: a mosaic of basic views and assumptions expressed as beliefs, values, and characteristic patterns of behavior shared by key members of the organization.*

*Why needed: to cope with internal and external pressures of a constantly evolving organization.*

Five factors influence the strength of an organizational culture and its resistance or receptivity to adaptation. They are:

1. The impact of the founder and his or her legacy
2. A similarity in views and the stability of group membership
3. The degree of employee commitment to overall goals and procedures
4. The degree of organizational conflict and distrust
5. A climate of growth or stagnation

## The Impact of the Founder

We saw at Disney that a major influence on an organizational culture is the impact of its founder and the founder's legacy. Many well-known companies, in fact, trace their culture back to influential founders who epitomize a particular value system. Thomas J. Watson, Sr., of IBM, Walt Disney at Disney, or Sir Henry Deterding, the founder of Royal Dutch Shell are some of the better-known examples.

Founders establish the tone of an organization, shaping its goals, aspirations, and operating maxims. Through behavior and policy, subsequent managements perpetuate the legacy.[6] Unfortunately, a founder's original concept of what made the business a success may eventually become a major obstacle to adaptation and change. What originally made sense sometimes becomes anachronistic, and founders' values and policies begin reflecting only what worked in the past.

In 1987, for example, four-time Boston Marathon winner Bill Rodgers saw the assets of his runner's apparel business seized by the Bank of Boston. Though Rodgers' name is legendary among runners, the market for runner's apparel dropped off dramatically in the five years since he began doing business. Rodgers' name and its mystique could no longer sell his company's old product in so glutted and discount-oriented a market. "It was a classic shake-out," Rob Yahn, the company president, told the *Boston Globe*, "where everybody had too many goods for too long."[7]

Yet the firm continued to rely on the founder's reputation, products, and methods to sell higher-priced items no longer desirable in the new market. Because of Rodgers' impressive credentials, his firm never considered major changes in their original vision.

## Like vs. Unlike Minds: Similarity in Group Views

Generally, a diversity in beliefs, values, and behavior makes it relatively easy to change an organizational culture. It engenders less monolithic, group-supported resistance to adaptation and more willingness to discuss different ideas. Many advertising agencies tend to embrace this healthy dynamic: Projects and executive behavior are always in flux and depend on a constant supply of creative inputs.

However, in a uniform culture, once the initial, fairly strong resistance is overcome, it may be easy to obtain consensus and a commitment to change. Such a state of affairs is naturally enhanced if group membership is stable. Observe how quickly the Disney turnaround took place once a strong leader (Eisner) settled in and provided long-needed leadership. In diverse groups, on the other hand, there will be more of an initial disposition to change—but gaining consensus and commitment for the actual implementation may be more difficult. We see this in detached firms where fragmentation prevents meaningful collaboration. Recall the hopelessly divided Société Générale, which only after many years began to adapt itself to changing realities.

The similarity and stability of uniform cultures is very much based on the intensity of the shared experiences of the group. This may be reinforced by organizational myths, legends, sagas, and stories (as in Hoover's FBI and at Disney). Such oral history is handed down to subsequent generations of employees and instills commitment to unique institutional values. The subsequent ideologies are sometimes established by dramatic leaders and carried out by compulsive or depressive ones who succeed them. Until Michael Eisner's arrival, this was unmistakably the case at Disney.

## Fitting In: Degree of Commitment to Company Goals

Do the members of the organization agree about the type of employee who really "fits"? Are members in unanimous accord about company strategies and policies? Although consensus concerning all these elements may make for unanimously pursued goals, shared zeal, and enthusiasm, as in dramatic and compulsive firms, it can also create rigid adherence to the values and policies of the leader or the "founding father," fostering both outdated strategies and structures (as at Disney). Too strong a commitment, then, to overall company goals and operating procedures may preclude the sort of constructive criticism that often leads to adaptive change. Remember the "bullying" that went on at Texas Instruments, where pleasing the bosses became more important than solving problems.

## Trust Me: Degree of Conflict and Distrust

The degree of conflict and distrust in the organization is another potential blockade to adaptation. As with the second-tier opportunism of the detached Société Générale, conflict and distrust can sometimes render executives amenable to actions that are at odds with overall company goals. Also, lack of trust and the presence of conflict fragment change efforts, requiring much time to reestablish channels of communication. We noted this in the tremendous upheaval at Sotheby's.

In climates of trust and cooperation, once the desirability of change is acknowledged, adaptation can be better orchestrated. A higher degree of member commitment allows communication to flow more easily. One caution, however: It may actually take longer for desired changes to be implemented in a trusting environment, since satisfaction can induce complacency.

## Grow or Give It Up: Climates of Growth or Stagnation

Growth and expansion programs that constantly require new staff members lead to climates of creative conflict. These enhance adaptability and encourage change. Managers seek shared values, trying harder to reach common goals and operating procedures.

In contrast, climates of stagnation foster conformity, unhealthy comfort zones, and resistance to adaptation. We noted this especially in firms suffering from depressive periods, notably A&P, Allis-Chalmers, and Melville Shoe.

# Organizational Blockades

We now discuss seven organizational blockades, or barriers, to adaptation. These must, of course, be noticed to be eliminated. They include:

1. Bureaucracy
2. Information systems
3. Distribution of power
4. Overexplicit planning
5. Narrow goals and strategies
6. Past success
7. Resource availability

## Where Rules Rule: Bureaucrats, Routines, and Clod Squads

There is obvious value in bureaucratic rules and regulations. They make operations run more smoothly and efficiently. Routine tasks get accomplished in an expedient way. But often too many rules create a pervasive climate in which nothing gets accomplished without an explicit procedure. Organizations function like preprogrammed machines, recalling our depressive and compulsive types: Everything routine gets handled in a routine way; everything else is ignored.

When new competitors and customer habits make change necessary, managers don't notice because their attention is focused inward. At Eastern Airlines, Rickenbacker changed little while his competition changed a lot—and as a consequence began taking away his market. He continued offering spartan services long after the markets no longer wanted them. He had instituted rules and they were followed to the detriment of the organization and its need for change. J. Edgar Hoover's subordinates took the philosopy of blind adherence to authority to the extreme, as did Avery's.

When changes in the marketplace are eventually noticed, bureaucratic managers may even then feel it is not worth adapting to them. It is very expensive to change elaborate rules and programs. Also, change creates inefficiency, something that is anathema to most compulsive organizations.

Another problem with bureaucratic rules is that they may sap the initiative of the workers and managers who must follow them. Alvin Gouldner in his *Patterns of Industrial Bureaucracy* has suggested that rules increase members' knowledge of "minimum acceptable behavior," ultimately compromising performance.[8] When sensible departures from the rules are punished, blind adherence becomes the order of the day. A mindless bureaucratic perspective comes to dominate. Thus lower-level managers tend to suppress any ideas they might have for constructive change, a real danger in compulsive and depressive organizations.

With too many rules, customers suffer, too: their wishes are slotted into only, at best, a few options. Special needs are completely ignored. Consider Eastern and TI's clients, who got only what the firms wanted to give them. Emerging tastes and promising new niches of the market are ignored. Henry Ford's only color scheme remained black.

In some bureaucracies managers delegate authority to improve their control over operations, setting up specialized subunits, each with its own functions. This can create competing departments whose goals come to take precedence over those of the organization. Société Générale gave us an example of this: Divisions in the company operated as uncooperative fiefdoms pursuing their goals at the expense of the overall organization. Resources gravitated to the most powerful divisions rather than the more promising, profitable ones. Performance declined precipitously.

### Suggestions:

Bureaucracy is hard to fight. Some firms have tried organizational development programs, task forces, and training seminars to evaluate company rules with a view toward eliminating those which hamper creative management; suggestion boxes to achieve the same end; incentive programs for innovative ideas; and employee surveys. But note: These are mere window dressing without a commitment to identify and combat unnecessary rules, regulations, and procedures. And that commitment must be supported by the top.

## Up a Blind Alley: Information Systems

Information systems are meant to inform managers about relevant trends inside and outside the firm. Managerial accounting systems tell managers how well the firm is doing through cost breakdowns and profit-and-loss statements. Informal components of the information system also gather softer data from outside the organization. Sales personnel, for example, may report the reactions of customers to new products; suppliers may interest the firm in a new manufacturing technique; newly recruited engineers might introduce a novel technology; and managers at trade associations may discover a strategy that a competitor is pursuing.

All of this information is grist for the decision-making mill. All things being equal, some believe that the more sophisticated and sensitive these information systems, the more adaptive the firm. Unfortunately, however, many information systems blind managers rather than enlighten them. One electronics firm we studied, the Klim Company (name disguised), had the most detailed cost accounting system imaginable, using it to identify production inefficiencies and shave costs to the bone.

But the company president, Sandra Klim, never seriously considered switching to more advanced microchips, as her firm's competitors had begun doing. These chips, because of their increased capacities, were yielding steadily higher profit margins. But Klim focused on costs rather than opportunities. As a result, the Klim Company had to slash the prices of its antiquated products just to keep up with the highly competitive market. The firm had become efficient in the production of goods no one wanted.

Unfortunately, information systems are usually a product of the views that existed when they were first designed. They often reflect past conditions, ideologies, and objectives, not current ones. They thus can present an antiquated picture of the firm's performance and its major challenges. Like the Klim Company, they may focus on data no longer usable, offering a false sense of security.

### Suggestion:

Annual evaluation of the firm's information system via a series of meetings between the accounting, R&D, production, and sales and marketing departments. Does the system enlighten management about emerging trends? This question must be imposed regularly. The relevance of reports must be questioned by recipients empowered to change them.

## Balancing Act: Distribution of Power

When power in the organization is tightly centralized, as in dramatic, compulsive, and suspicious firms, the individual who holds it can become a bottleneck who stymies adaptation in the face of unanimous opposition. This is especially true when power accrues only to a personality or position rather than to knowledge. Who would dare to try forcing a Rickenbacker or an Avery to alter his strategies?

Where the top executive is a dramatic, entrepreneurial personality, too much change and even recklessness will be *facilitated* by centralization. Cornfeld, De Lorean, Ash, Thornton, and others could hardly be dissuaded from their revolutionary changes. They held all the power—formal as well as charismatic. Thus, extreme centralization will cause major shifts in the degree of change.[9]

But there is a difference between change and adaptation. While powerful managers can implement a great deal of change, this does not mean their changes will be adaptive. In dramatic firms, managers are powerful and create cultures in which they will be idealized by their subordinates. Unfortunately, a dramatic's often insular perspective is the only one likely to influence decisions. So the organization fails to benefit from the multiple points of view of middle managers. This makes a balanced picture unlikely and reduces adaptivity, even in a changing organization.

Balance, however, is hard to come by. While over-centralization can thwart adaptation, so can too much decentralization. The very broad distribution of power to lower-level units that we noted in the detached Société Générale also stifled adaptivity. Chiefs of the feuding subunits possessed so much power, the overall organization lacked direction. Subunits operated as independent fiefdoms.

Such decentralization sometimes facilitates small, interdepartmental changes, since there is no felt need to consult with other departments or to get things approved "upstairs."

But when a major, concerted, organization-wide change in a decentralized firm becomes necessary, things bog down. Subunits are unused to the idea of collaborating with one another, and distrust and political interests destabilize the subordinates' incentive to contribute to overall organizational goals. Most damaging of all, no central authority exists to pull these feuding subunits together.

### *Suggestion:*

Constant vigilance and an awareness of the abuses of power—the checks and balances. An outside consultant can evaluate how well the firm is achieving its balance; typically, more delegating will be needed by those with dramatic, compulsive, and suspicious slants, stronger and more centralized decision-making by those of the detached and depressive school, respectively. Often, only someone from outside the firm can be objective enough to make the diagnosis.

## The Illusion of Invincibility: Overexplicit Planning

Having a vision for the future and formulating action plans can sometimes be taken too far, as we have seen in compulsive firms. There is real danger that the organization will attempt to program the future, to devise hardened and detailed long-term plans that allow too little freedom and permit almost no reassessment. Such plans ignore reality as the need for control begins to dominate everything. The view of the environment becomes what one wishes rather than what is. Programs supplant evaluation; implementation replaces adaptation.

At Redfield's Itel, for example, the dream of a magnificent conglomerate outweighed the hard results of how much success the implementation of the dream was generating.

Adaptation was lacking as the firm backed into the future with its antiquated model of the world.

**Suggestion:**
Constant updating of master plans; semiannual weekend retreats for the executive group to reevaluate company goals; a suspicion of targets more than two years old; constant appraisal of past plans.

## Myopic Visions: Narrow Goals and Strategies

Some organizations conceive of their mission in such a restricted way that it soon becomes out of date. Myopic firms, especially compulsive and depressive ones, rarely recognize the need for change. Their narrow focus makes them fail to see that their orientation is no longer relevant.

Henry Ford, for example, was the last to see the defects in his Model T. Garber and Stone designed its strategy to beautifully fit a staid, conservative, narrow market—a market that had died. Bill Rodgers' reliance only on runners' clothing limited his enterprise's possibilities.

In short, narrowly focused objectives make things easier in the short run, producing concrete targets toward which a firm can work. But ultimately they may foster blindness and inhibit flexibility.

**Suggestion:**
Creation of alternative master plans and scenarios about the mission of the firm and its future; contingency plans; discussion of corporate evolutionary paths, long-range goals, market threats and opportunities, and possibilities for diversification.

## Why Change? The Hidden Danger of Past Success

"Nothing succeeds like success" goes the old adage. Yet very often success sows the seeds of outright failure. Disney, we noted, went through a period in which its managers were reluctant to tamper with tried-and-true formulas—and there were painful, disastrous consequences.

Managers who design a successful strategy become identified with it and often derive their reputation, prestige, and even power from it. Henry Ford created the Model T, which at one time could not have been more successful. Cornfeld gave extraordinary life to IOS.

Such managers, however, are loath to admit when their creation no longer represents the best way of doing things. They resist becoming a party to its demise. Organizations are complex entities. Since no one can be sure what it is about a strategy that has made it successful, only reluctantly do managers make even incremental changes. Any change, it is surmised, might destroy the synergy of the original package.

After a long period of success firms have an almost infinite ability to rationalize away what they perceive to be short-term declines in performance. "Anomalous" conditions in the environment are said to have caused "temporary" difficulties. Ford, Rickenbacker, and Cornfeld had been spectacularly successful: Why change horses in midstream just because of a temporary setback. Strategies proven useful for so long, under so broad a variety of past conditions, can't be all bad, these managers reason.

So why change?

### Suggestion:

Try the "Two-Quarter Bounce-Off"—if an unexpected decline continues for more than one quarter, hold special sessions to allow top managers to bounce ideas off one another and critically evaluate present strategy, information systems, distribution of power, and other items on our list of organizational blockades. This will work only if the toughest questions are asked in a climate allowing a free exchange of ideas.

## Slack for the System: Resource Availability

Adaptation and change are expensive. Human and capital resources of considerable magnitude are required. When such resources are not available, options for change become extremely limited.

Without slack in the system there will be little room for experimentation. This may be a particular problem in a dramatic organization where too much action has depleted organizational resources, or in the depressive firm where so much inaction has caused the same result.

Before too long, for example, De Lorean's and Cornfeld's expenditures of financial resources were beyond salvaging; Patterson's extravagance gave his bank still less time to reach this point of no return.

### Suggestions:
Keep track of the flow of resources; calculate margins of safety. How many failures of a given magnitude can be tolerated? What is the worst case scenario?

Again, an outside consultant may be brought in to evaluate the firm's financial resources and recommend what kind of strategic plan is realistic; an outsider might also evaluate "soft" areas such as "team spirit" and company morale, making recommendations for the commitment of human energy.

## Barriers to Adaptation by Neurotic Type

In our five troubled types of firms, the blockades we have just discussed exist in abundance and hamper even the most strenuous remedial efforts.

But there is much that can be done about them. In the following section, we suggest programs that make each of the types more adaptive. These are not panaceas. Their practicality depends on individual circumstances. Our programs address these barriers as they occur—in combinations that disclose more fundamental organizational problems. Combatting obstacles singly, although sometimes helpful, will never be entirely effective. Always, the *roots* of the pathology must be addressed, not the symptoms.

## Dramatic Firms: Planting Both Feet Firmly on the Ground

Dominated by their dynamic, charismatic leader, the subordinates in a dramatic firm adopt unquestioning attitudes, allowing the leader to commit to foolish and risky projects. Also, a climate of growth and expansion and the high level of commitment to goals results in a uniform and "dependent" culture. So boldness in the pursuit of the idealized leader's objectives is common.

Unfortunately, adaptation that requires a more analytical orientation—a reduction in risk-taking, a reassessment and consolidation of strategy—is very hard to initiate. Power is at the top, so lower-level managers find it difficult to exert pressure to change. Too little information is gathered, so top executives fail to recognize the need for action. Often, past success, especially rapid growth, makes dramatic leaders extremely reluctant to abandon earlier commitments. Adaptation is stymied by strategies that are uncodified and informal. No explicit plans exist to serve as objects of criticism or discussion. Most plans simply reside in the mind of the CEO.

### Stabilization:

What dramatic companies need above all is stability. Both the organization's feet need to be planted firmly on the ground. Alfred Sloan brought this to General Motors as he tried to neutralize some of the effects of the frenetically expansionary Durant regime: GM's deterioration had become an emergency when a slump in the national economy in 1920 caused the bottom to drop out of the automobile market. This, and a lack of control over operations, led to Durant's resignation. His informal ways of doing business and his unwillingness to deal with organizational matters had led to myriad inefficiencies.

According to Sloan, Durant had "expanded General Motors between 1918 and 1920 without an explicit policy of management with which to control the various parts of the organization."[10] His impulsive way of making decisions, combined with the depressive state of the economy, brought the company to the brink.

Sloan was appointed the prime mover to handle the crisis. A plan drafted by him a year earlier under the unassuming title "Organization Study" became the basis for a sweeping reorganization, and indeed the foundation of a new management philosophy. His new organizational design was guided by the wish to find a stable, happy medium between the extremes of decentralization and pure centalization. Although each division would have a considerable amount of discretion, new central organizational functions were introduced to control the activities of the overall corporation. This began with the formation of an executive committee to set policy.

After a transitional period Sloan took over as president in 1923. To coordinate all activities he introduced a number of committees other than the executive. The interdivisional relations committees dealt with functional areas such as purchasing, engineering, and sales. An operating committee formed to appraise the performance of the divisions. Sophisticated controls and information systems were adopted. This new scheme of management became the foundation for a new General Motors, transforming the company from an agglomeration of different business units into a single, coordinated enterprise. As Alfred Chandler states in his book, *Strategy and Structure*; "The new organizational structure served General Motors well. From 1924 to 1927, the corporation's share of the motor vehicle market rose from 10.8 to 43.3 percent. In the following year its profits stood at an impressive $276,468,000. From then on, General Motors has maintained the leading position in the industry."[11]

In short, dramatic firms benefit from consolidation, decentralization, and tighter administration. The flow of information must be opened up, new leaders developed, and discussion and disagreement encouraged. Because dramatic CEOs are so powerful and forceful, they are unlikely to be willing to undertake these changes unless they—the board of directors or their shareholders—can be convinced of the serious consequences of their strategies. Too often, this requires some tangible, if painful, evidence of poor performance. To gain some time, change agents must make a very strong case against the costs of dramatic behavior.

## Suspicious Firms: Back to the Future

The suspicious firm has a group culture rife with distrust, fear, and suspicion. Anyone with an "aberrant" point of view is suspect and gotten rid of. Such a uniform culture enforces one view of the environment—of customers, the competition, everything. This gets in the way of any objective analysis of external conditions and suppresses crucial information. "Group think" becomes the norm. Timely and sensible adaptation may be thwarted.

The suspicious leader also centralizes power and has all kinds of information flowing to the top. Suspicious leaders make all key decisions themselves, certain that no one else in the organization can really be trusted. Obsessed with enemies both inside and outside the firm, their perceptions (and information systems) quickly become so biased that key trends are missed regularly and selective events are met with overreaction. Implementation of change may also be impeded by suspicion and conflict. Finally, a preoccupation with competitors thwarts the emergence of a distinctive, integrated strategy.

### Looking Ahead

Given their obsession with threats, loyalty, and betrayal, suspicious executives spend too much of their time analyzing and reacting to the initiatives of others and not enough time on creative programs and concerted strategies. They need to develop a more integrated and thematic strategy to allow their firms to build distinctive competences. And it is necessary to allow and encourage dissent and to provoke more frank discussions.

In 1982 a Wall Street analyst, referring to ITT's generally sluggish earnings performance said, "Harold Geneen was an absolute disaster as an operating manager. You have only to look at the record—he could acquire companies but he could not manage them. And his further failing was that he couldn't recognize this."[12] Geneen's successors now want the company to return to its core business, and its area of competence, telecommunications. But some industry analysts believe this will be an uphill battle given the company's liquidity problems. Unfortunately, Geneen's emphasis on acquisitions and his passion for quarterly earnings gains has left ITT with a very high debt-to-equity ratio.[13]

Suspicious firms need infusions of participation, trust, openness, more unified strategies, and a sense of mission that is relevant to external markets. Generally they can achieve these radical transformations only after the departure of the old CEO.

## Detached Firms: Please Step Aside

A withdrawn, cold, and vacillating leader opens a firm to much politicking. CEOs fail to give direction to their executives and interfere only inconsistently and sporadically. So the business must be run largely by the second tier, who strive to get the attention of the CEO. Many are game players who jockey for power and try to fill the leadership vacuum, making coordination difficult and blocking the implementation of significant change. Parochial, departmental thinking dominates, as at Société Générale, inhibiting the emergence of one concerted, unifying strategy.

### Coping

As we mentioned in Chapter 4, occasionally an executive's withdrawal from decision-making will actually permit a fragmented organization to operate more smoothly. This is one way, albeit an incomplete one, of solving the problems of a detached firm. Even before his mental breakdown, for example, Howard Hughes, who inherited Hughes Tool from his entrepreneur father, had been erratic in running the business. Hughes' top executives complained constantly in the forties and fifties of his poor supervisory capabilities, his inability to make up his mind, and, even then, of his reclusiveness. After a walkout of some eighty top scientists, engineers, and managers at Hughes Aircraft, Harold Talbot, secretary of the Air Force in 1953, went so far as to tell Hughes to his face: "You've made a hell of a mess of a great property, and by God, so long as I am Secretary of the Air Force, you're not going to get another dollar of new business."[14] This may, in fact, have helped to induce Hughes to withdraw from Hughes Aircraft, bringing his management of the firm to the level of that at Hughes Tool, where he never interfered. His attention shifted toward other ventures.

Lawrence "Pat" Hyland, president of Hughes Aircraft since 1954, never found the continued detached behavior of Mr. Hughes to be a serious problem throughout two decades. "No, I don't get upset when I can't get through to him," he explained to a reporter in 1968. "I send my plans along to him, and if I don't hear from him, and they still seem reasonable to me, I go ahead with them. We have a very productive partnership—it is an unorthodox kind of relationship and I don't know of any parallel, but it fits very well."[15]

Hyland represents one of those rare second-tier executives who can fill the void of a boss's withdrawal. Indeed, a major opportunity in some detached forms is to sidestep the leader. A promising second-tier executive can be promoted to a group vice-president or general manager's position that allows the firm to have a new de facto leader. Truly detached CEOs often welcome this opportunity, as it frees more of their time.

## Depressive Firms: Turning the Queen Mary

Depressive firms are beset by a malaise that gets in the way of any key change, adaptive or not. The manager at the top just doesn't care enough to do much. A climate of stagnation ensues and spreads the malaise at the top down to lower levels. For the most part, things remain the same.

Appeals for change in a depressive firm are simply ignored until activist managers become resigned to the status quo. A "muddling through" approach symbolizes lack of commitment to anything. The bureaucracy and resistance to change interfere with communication, and morale plummets. Ultimately, inaction saps the firm's resources via the erosion of market shares and profits. In many instances executives in depressive firms feel like pawns in a game over which they have very little control. This will be the case in situations of takeovers where the dominant firm is imposing its way of doing things on the other company without room for consultation.

### Saving Depressives

Without a transformation of the depressive style of management, there can be no alternative for depressive companies than to continue their decline. The depressive executive's world view—that human action can do little to improve things—is a formidable obstacle. If the depressive outlook is deeply embedded in the CEO's psyche, change is difficult. If, on the other hand, environmental impositions caused the depressive outlook of the executive group, change will be easier. If we are dealing with the former, the depressive state of the firm can usually be changed only by a new corps of executives.

A classic example involves United Airlines' Edward Carlson, who took over from George Keck in 1971 and completely revitalized the firm. Carlson immediately embarked on an ambitious, multifaceted, hard-driving campaign, spreading decision-making throughout the depressive firm's ranks, paring down a bloated top executive staff, slashing company payrolls, and "pressing flesh" with both customers and workers on the line. Carlson even asked personnel at all levels for their opinions, and he listened!

The result? Only one year later, United found itself back as a real threat to its competition for the first time in five years. Carlson's approach brought the airline's costs way down, while revenues began edging back up. Even United's deficit, a problem for many years, fell dramatically under Carlson's new regime.[16]

As mentioned, sometimes a takeover of a firm by another firm contributes to a depressive culture, but it may also breathe new life into a stagnant firm. Lackluster performance and a depressed share price sometimes make depressed companies prime takeover candidates. And often the takeover is accompanied by new management that revitalizes the company.

One executive with A&P declared bravely during the late sixties, "It takes longer to turn around the *Queen Mary* than it does a rowboat," implying that his company, somehow, someday, might make it back to the top under the existing orientation. But the truth seems closer to the comment of a Wall Street analyst, who wrote, in reaction to the executive's comparison, "Some A&P critics think the comparison is foreboding. The *Queen Mary,* once lord of the seas, now is moored in Long Beach, California, as a museum relic of a bygone age."[17]

In fact, A&P's continued lackluster performance did eventually lead to a takeover. In 1979 the German Tengelman Group, a big family-owned European food retailer, took control over the then third-largest food chain in the nation. And it has since brought new life to the company by installing new managers who have been quite successful in introducing innovative merchandising techniques. Many wonder, however, if the company will ever regain its old glory.[18]

Where the depressive culture is caused by circumstance—declining markets, a takeover—it can sometimes be reversed by diversification into new areas and innovative projects. This can create vigor and a sense of hope, as was the case at Disney with the arrival of former Paramount executive Michael Eisner. Eisner founded Touchstone Pictures, which presented the first-ever Disney "R" rated movies, including *Splash* and *Outrageous Fortune.* Addressing new challenges and problems that are solvable tends to erode a sense of helplessness, and sometimes also generates enthusiasm and confidence. Action combats depression.

## Compulsive Firms: Waging the Battle Against Control

The theme in the compulsive firm, as we learned earlier, is clearly "rigidity." The compulsive firm may be wed to the ideas, policies, and strategies of a departed founder or present leader. It has evolved a highly routinized way of doing things. Too much attention is devoted to details as critical new challenges and opportunities are ignored. The elaborate, rigid structures are costly to change, strategy is hopelessly narrow, and goals are too explicit. The need to adapt is rarely recognized.

The emphasis in compulsive firms is on tending a well-oiled machine and forcing things to fit preestablished molds. Compulsive companies often track efficiency rather than effectiveness, their elaborate information systems keeping managers focused on the wrong issues. Their systems provide internal information about things like scrap rates and costs per unit but tell nothing of environmental trends that demand change.

### Flexibility walk

Only when executives combat rigidity in their attitudes, open themselves to broader issues inside and outside the firm, and embrace change will true innovation, adaptability, and versatility become possible. Ironically, because they have such excellent controls, compulsive firms quickly realize that they are in trouble: They know when costs are out of control, when margins are shrinking, and when market shares are declining.

Managers can play upon this, demonstrating the costs of narrow tradition and rigidity and suggesting improvements—innovations, modes of diversification—that can be adopted incrementally. This allows compulsive CEOs to believe their favorite strategies are not being abandoned—but only broadened. It enables them to use their treasured controls in monitoring the new ventures. And it creates an opportunity for promoting promising new managers to newly formed positions. But compulsives will never tolerate dramatic departures from the status quo.

Unfortunately, compulsive executives sometimes resist *all* changes, and adaptation must await their departure. Melville Shoe, Eastern Airlines, Ford, and Ward's changed only after Melville, Rickenbacker, Ford, and Avery, respectively, left.

Table 2:
Barriers and Passages to Adaptation by Organizational Type

| *Type* | *Barriers* | *Needs* |
|---|---|---|
| Dramatic Firms | Domineering leader/ founder | Distribution of authority and grooming of talented second-tier managers |
| | Zealous, unquestioning commitment by managers to idolized leader and the leader's objectives | Codification of strategy |
| | | Establishment of clear reporting hierarchy |
| | Climate of growth for its own sake, abundant vigor | Coordinative committees, and controls |
| | Poor or overloaded information systems that fail to reveal underlying weaknesses | Scanning of the environment |
| | Power resides with the charismatic leader; extremely centralized | |
| | No clear plans except, perhaps, in the mind of leader | |
| | Past success encourages recklessness and climate of obedience | |

| Type | Barriers | Needs |
|------|----------|-------|
| Suspicious Firms | Fears and suspicion induce great uniformity of values and beliefs, narrowing points of view | Fostering an attitude of trust by breaking down communication barriers |
| | Conflict and distrust prevent effective communication and collaboration | Participative culture |
| | | Pursuit of strategic themes |
| | Information systems formal and sophisticated but designed around pet fears, ignoring other, perhaps more important, information | Pursuit of strategic themes and foci |
| | | Creation of distinctive competencies |
| | Suspicion causes power to be centralized at the top, resulting in too little grass-roots adaptation | |
| Detached Firms | Major differences among unstable, opportunistic departmental factions. Much conflict generated by such differences | A new leader, or a key second-tier executive who takes the leader's role |
| | The firm's inner conflicts worsened by a lack of leadership, de facto power often falling into the hands of feuding factions | Better coordinative committees |
| | Concerted plans nonexistent | Incentives that reward for overall organizational performance and discourage parochial interests |
| | Communcations and collaborations thwarted by conflict | |

| *Type* | *Barriers* | *Needs* |
|---|---|---|
| Depressive Firms | A malaise reduces commitment to goals; apathy prevails | New leadership |
| | A climate of stagnation aggravates the firm's apathy, preventing acting on felt needs to adapt | Financing to undertake strategic reorientation and renewal |
| | | Pruning of unpromising ventures |
| | Bureaucracy and automatic procedures blind managers to the "big picture" | Search for opportunities in markets via scanning. |
| | Planning is rare; firm drifts along aimlessly | |
| | Malaise and lack of direction make collaboration difficult | |
| | Resources are depleted by the lack of adaptation, further restricting options for change | |
| Compulsive Firms | Founder may have left a "bible" that is followed slavishly and mindlessly | Creativity seminars |
| | Preoccupations of leader are followed dogmatically | Change of selection practice; |
| | | Openness to lower-level suggestions |
| | Bureaucracy causes resistance to change | Scanning of markets for problems and opportunities |
| | Plans so explicit as to admit almost no flexibility | |
| | Goals and strategies very narrow; key problems and opportunities neglected totally | |

## Chapter Nine

# Organizational Intervention: A Case Study

**W**hen Judith Singer first took the job of vice-president of finance and accounting at Orion Corporation, a manufacturer/ distributor of paper products, her first major assignment was to set up a new cost accounting and budgeting system. She had conceived the idea herself after inspecting the old system and noting how outdated it had become. Orion was currently experiencing a boom—its president, Douglas Pizzi, had embarked on an ambitious expansion and diversification program and sales had reached the $100 million mark. When Singer pointed out the antiquated accounting and budgeting system to Pizzi, he wanted a new system developed immediately.

After Singer installed her system, however, she discovered Orion was losing money. Never before in the company's history had this happened—or if it had, no one had ever reported or discovered it. But Singer's new budgeting system had disclosed some problems.

President Pizzi did not take this information lightly. To Singer's surprise, Pizzi blamed *her* for the company's losses. "You took much too long implementing your new system," Pizzi exclaimed. "Everything's been in chaos for months because of it. We haven't even been able to keep track of what's been going on." Pizzi added that Singer's new system was too complex. Later, to others, he wondered aloud whether he had not made a mistake by hiring a woman for such an important position.

Singer believed that the real reasons for the losses were not the budgeting system but the cost overruns, grandiose expenditures, and faulty purchasing decisions they disclosed. She reported this to Pizzi, but he just wouldn't listen. Soon after, Singer found herself routinely excluded from the decision-making process.

Our final step in exploring neurotic firms presents an example of what we do when we intervene in an organization. We offer this as a guide so that readers might better understand similar problems in their own organizations. Before beginning, however, we must caution that interventions cannot take place casually. Only when there is an active commitment to change from the powerholder(s) of an organization in question will there be a chance of success. Also, since insiders can develop "tunnel vision," outside consultants can sometimes make a useful contribution.

Orion Corporation had begun as a converter of paper products in the fifties and for a long time remained a simple manufacturer of paper boxes. During that period, sales stabilized at $20 million and net profits ran constant at about $1 million. Then, in 1971, due to poor health, Orion's founder, Robert Van Buren, decided to go public and sell most of his stock. The current president, Doug Pizzi, had been with the company for eight years by then, having sold his own company, which produced decorative wrapping and ribbons, to Orion.

Part of the deal was that Pizzi stay on to run his old company. But his success in doing so was so great that when the Orion founder stepped down a few years later, he asked Pizzi to take over the company.

We first came into contact with Orion when vice-president Singer called us, mentioning she was actually calling on behalf of the president, who wanted some help in strategic planning and in setting up a formal human-resource management system. "Our company has grown rapidly over the past five years," Singer told us. "It's becoming more and more difficult to control our operations. There are now so many of them."

On our first visit to the company's main facility in a relatively rundown urban area, we were struck by the contrast between the gleaming eight-story square building with its shimmering glass facade and the dilapidated walk-up apartments and storefronts on either side of the street. While the dingy storefronts displayed faded swatches of fabrics and unwashed windows, a magnificent modern tapestry adorned the Orion reception area across the lobby from four stainless-steel elevator doors. It was only on the fourth floor, amid the din of heavy machinery, that we remembered what kind of business Orion really was.

In a corner of the work area, we saw two well-dressed buyers laughing and partaking of chocolate-dipped strawberries. Their host, a gracious, hefty middle-aged man, turned out to be Doug Pizzi, Orion's president. "Glad you could come," Pizzi greeted us, shaking our hands vigorously and inviting into his office.

After coffee and preliminaries, Pizzi brought out a number of recent Orion financial reports and we spent the next hour perusing them. As we read and asked questions, we began to learn that over the last three years, from 1983 to 1986, Orion had had an extremely erratic record of profits. Pizzi offered many reasons for this checkered record, but it appeared that a critical factor had been his ambitious expansions into related paper products. To its traditional paper boxes and holiday paper lines, Pizzi had added stationery, business forms, and envelopes. These items became Orion's biggest sellers, accounting for more than 60 percent of its sales.

More recently, a new venture had been started as well, in napkins and paper towels. Plans were also under way to enter facial and bathroom tissue markets and to supply reams of copier paper to manufacturers of copy machines.

In 1984, Pizzi also embarked on a program to "consolidate" and modernize Orion's facilities. From this venture evolved the huge eight-story complex. Pizzi had made the decision to build this complex in spite of the warnings of a consulting firm Orion had hired for feasibility studies. Consultants noted logistical problems in the neighborhood, high labor costs, troubled labor-management relations, and uncertain economic prospects for the near future.

Yet of the five senior executives, only one supported the consultants' recommendations. The other executives concurred with Pizzi's plans to go ahead despite the dire projections. The consultants were fired.

The resulting major "consolidation," or more appropriately, expansion, doubled the size of the production plant and offices. The changeover proved far more costly and disruptive than originally expected: There were major production and delivery problems and the company soon found itself with excess capacity. It was also discovered that Orion was headed for a sizable loss in 1985. The firm, once so cash-rich, had now become entirely dependent on its banks.

Responding to our request to describe his managerial style, Pizzi unflincingly characterized himself as a man easily excited. "But I'm a quick decision-maker as well, and I know what decisions need to be made," he added. "And I have damned little patience for incompetence." He went on, "Orion's current problems have really been the result of an unexpected depression. This industry currently is under attack: We've got high interest rates against us, cheap imports, and excessive demands from our unions."

Pizzi also noted two of his most recently hired executives had turned out to be big disappointments. "I'd say I'm too optimistic a guy!" he exclaimed. "And too trusting! I gave both these new hires a little too much credit, I guess. I miscalculated their abilities and experience. They both failed miserably at making a success of the new ventures I gave them to handle."

Pizzi swiveled around in his red leather executive's chair behind his ornate Queen Anne desk and gazed out the window. A huge trailer truck was wheeling down the narrow street to pick up a load of Orion orders. "Of course, I know I'm ultimately responsible for everything that goes on around here, I do realize that. But you know, I can't do it all myself, I really can't. I need more initiative from my managers."

A moment later, he picked up one of the thicker financial reports and held it a minute, slowly shaking his head. "That new budgeting system Singer installed," he said, "just took far too long to get going. While we waited for it, I had to get along with a minimum of managerial information and a total lack of cost figures I could count on."

Pizzi recounted other problems as well: too many employees added much too quickly, with the predictable adjustment problems; start-up costs of the many new operations that "soared off the charts"; new executives who made "colossal mistakes." Yet in spite of all his setbacks, Pizzi remained optimistic about Orion's future. "Our problems at Orion are only temporary," he declared. "I see so many exciting new opportunities coming across my desk every day that I just can't contain myself. Why, right now for example, I'm looking into the possibility of marketing novelty pencils!"

At this point in the intervention process with Orion we needed a better grasp of the minds, beliefs, and emotional lives of the company's top managers. So we attended Orion's executive sessions, observing interactions and personal styles. And we met individually with each of the important players— all the vice-presidents and several major department heads. We began probing these players: How did you come to Orion? Why? What excites you about your work here? What do you find frustrating? What does the future hold?

Eventually we go beyond the narrow parameters of work: How does life inside the company parallel your life outside? What are the conflicts? We also ask about personal relations, ambitions, interests, and family background. Our aim is to get a complete, dynamic picture of the interpersonal relations at work at our client company and how can we categorize them. Can we find, for example, dramatic, depressive, suspicious, detached, or compulsive elements or themes? Always, we emphasize that we will preserve confidentiality—that we are trying to compose an overall picture of the company. From there we can recommend forms of intervention.

During our interviews with some of Orion's executives, a number of issues came to the fore. In examining decision-making, for example, we were struck by the unplanned way in which a number of new divisions had been added to the company. It appeared that Orion embraced new divisions the way other firms added new products. Also, several key executives became preoccupied with "filling up" the spacious new facilities at any cost, even when this meant broaching unpromising and marginal markets.

We spoke with one of Pizzi's newly hired managers, Nancy Savoy, director of product management, who characterized Orion as a company where decision-makers "shot from the hip." Firefighting and management-by-crisis were Orion's rule. "When I was hired," she said, "I discovered President Pizzi had also assigned another executive to do almost exactly the same job. He left after a few months, but for a while it was ridiculously confusing. But that's the way life goes at Orion—confusion, frustration, sometimes bizarre allocations of responsibility. You never quite know what your job is and what it's not." Savoy added that Pizzi regularly used her as a sounding board to explore new ideas, but seemed to do so to the great irritation of her immediate superior.

Recently she had even begun wondering if Pizzi really

wanted honest feedback. "Too many times he seems interested in having his own ideas affirmed," she said. "Taking in other points of view seems the last thing on his mind."

Savoy also indicated her displeasure at Pizzi's way of motivating people. He would frequently scold them, for example, by remarking how well other managers were doing. This was a practice that infuriated everyone. So managers went to Pizzi with only good news, since he didn't take anything else very well. "He gets excited all right," commented Savoy, when told her leader's description of himself. "Give him bad news and he goes right through the roof!"

The result was predictable. Subordinates routinely painted too rosy a picture of things for Pizzi, leading to an atmosphere of false optimism.

Nancy Savoy was one of the few dissenting voices. But the reactions of most of the executives we spoke with, especially those who had been around far longer than Savoy, were quite different. Many talked enthusiastically of Orion's "sensational diversification program" and of the company's exciting new opportunities. One manager described his boss as a visionary who would one day make Orion "number one" in the entire paper products industry. We detected, however, a rather hollow, mechanical quality to such statements.

In an unusual display of candor, Pizzi's staff assistant, Danny Fay, began criticizing Orion's recently completed expansion-construction program. He said his boss had wanted to erect these new facilities for many years. Ultimately the program had resulted in a serious depletion of working capital. In Fay's opinion, the impact of the consolidation had been devastating: "We have a monster here that has to be fed! And now we can't ever scale down." Only when these new facilities were filled and production at full capacity again would Orion be able to make more money. In one of his frequent mythological references—he had been a Classics major at Cornell, he told us—Fay claimed the firm was "between Scylla and Charybdis."

"On the one hand, see, there was Pizzi's push to expand more. On the other hand, there's great inefficiency and a terrible loss of reserves. And it's hard for him to delegate responsibility, it's one of his toughest things! He's always got to get his hands on everything." Pizzi, Fay concluded, wasted a lot of his valuable time on trivial matters while paying too little attention to many of Orion's more key decisions.

"My feeling is that the man is just impossible to predict," he added. "He bypasses us all the time, bad news makes him panic, and he goes in fifty directions at once, giving 'urgent' orders right down to the shop-floor level."

Fay's final comments were illuminating: "You know, I don't sleep very well any longer because of him. It is just so difficult to work for this man. Of course, I could be just like the others and agree with everything he says, but I find I can't do that. He listens to what I say if he wants to hear it. If he doesn't, he gets me out of his office fast. Sometimes he actually comes down to my office and yells at me, supposedly because I have done something wrong. But then I am just the scapegoat of the moment. I hate to say it, but sometimes I feel like putting both hands around his neck and strangling the man."

## Making Sense of a Bad Situation

So what was the problem with Orion Corporation? There were many obvious organizational clues inviting inspection. So we took a look at the most visible ones first.

The company's organization chart, for example, was muddled and, in line with Savoy's comments, hopelessly confusing. In fact, several conflicting organization charts floated around the corporate offices. No clear lines divided responsibilities between product divisions and functional departments, and responsibility centers were nonexistent.

In talking to the many upper- and middle-level executives, we found that skirmishes over roles and prerogatives were the order of the day. Inevitably, such conflicts permeated to lower levels of management. Marketing research was being carried out halfheartedly, and there was very little competitive analysis in the company. The sales force was poorly organized, and some divisions even used sales agents who were pushing the lines of competitors. There were no performance reviews, and control systems were woefully inadequate, allowing many inefficiencies in operations to go undetected.

In spite of the modernization program, the various manufacturing facilities connected with one another poorly, making them highly inefficient. Labor relations were unsatisfactory and the organization of the work flow was inappropriate. Several of these problems were caused by the impulsive way in which the new divisions and products had been added.

It also became clear that given the company's size and complexity, decision-making gravitated too automatically toward Pizzi's desk. He seemed to be trying to run the whole show himself, meddling in routine divisional and departmental operating matters while at the same time making risky, bold, and dramatic decisions. As a result, he had little time left for formulating long-term strategies, monitoring and integrating the new ventures and acquisitions, getting involved in competitive analysis, and evaluating the product mix. Moreover, he failed to develop managerial talent to take some of the load off his shoulders. Strategies became downright conflicting, and reacting to crisis was the norm.

The erratic way in which new divisions had been added had also seriously depleted working capital, over and above the costs of the consolidation and modernization program. All these flaws made Orion more vulnerable to increasing competition while straining the firm's resources. They also invited scrutiny by increasingly skeptical creditors.

Many of Orion's problems were quite obvious. Almost any competent management consultant would have discovered them very quickly. But the question we were asking over and over was this: What made Pizzi act the way he did? And what was it about his style that had such a ripple effect throughout the company? Why did he build his white elephant of a headquarters and plant? And why did a climate of optimism persist in the company when in actuality things were going so badly?

## The Making of a President: Orion's Doug Pizzi

There was a joke going around the paper products industry that Douglas Pizzi suffered from a psychological disorder. They called it his "edifice complex." After all, he did so enjoy showing off his new facilities to all who came around. So at this point, we had to find out more about Pizzi the person.

We initiated relaxed and informal probing sessions—three of them, each four hours. The last two sessions took place in Pizzi's home, away from the bustle of the office. We asked Pizzi about his background, his professional history, his major failures and successes. The discussion had little structure and Pizzi was encouraged to do most of the talking.

It soon became clear his relationships with authority figures since childhood had been fraught with conflict. This might have originated with his ambivalent attitude toward a rather overbearing and controlling mother. "Every time I got into trouble," he told us one session, "my mother would tell me I'd never amount to anything." But not all his early experiences with his mother had been negative. There had been much love and encouragement as well.

Doug Pizzi had come to the United States as an immigrant from a poor village in Italy, and his first years in the new country had been very difficult for him—he had had to start all over again. His previous education and experience had seemed of little value. He'd been forced to live in a small apartment not far from Orion's current new facilities. He liked to tell anyone who would listen how hard it had been to hold on to a job in those days and how others used to see him as a complete failure. He'd then look around at his life and see people's characterizations of him as true: He was "nothing, a nobody who had never really accomplished anything." Perhaps this increased his need to demonstrate to the world—as when he was a child—that he could indeed amount to something.

Working for others was not easy for Doug Pizzi. Sometimes relationships with bosses in his earliest jobs worked out, but more often they didn't. Given such difficulties fitting into a more structured subordinate situation, he seized upon the opportunity to start his own company. Through hard work and ingenuity he built it up to a respectable enterprise and finally sold it to Orion. At the time, he also insisted that if he were to stay on as division head, he must have a completely free hand in making key decisions.

This organizational scenario provided by Pizzi seemed to indicate he felt he had not yet accomplished all he needed to. Even his eventual accession to the presidency of Orion had not been sufficient. He seemed to crave more glory, more attention. To boost his shaky self-esteem, he wanted still more of the limelight. We guessed that this partially explained his dramatic diversification program and his need to build the white-elephant edifice: both were tangible, ostentatious symbols of success in the business world. Seeing these decisions in the context of Pizzi's overall life history, the "irrational" acts of constructing new facilities and expanding at an inappropriate time and pace seemed understandable. It was even the same neighborhood where he had suffered many of his setbacks and disappointments. It was here that he wanted to show others just how far he had come.

## Intervention: What We Did

Given Pizzi's background and motivations and the ripple effect his leadership style was having on his organization, the question was, What steps could be taken to restore health to Orion?[1] How could we help Pizzi and his key executives to develop greater insight into the sources of Orion's problems? How much interpretation and insight were tolerable to the key players? Was there enough "pain" in the system to overcome the considerable personal, cultural, and organizational resistances to change?

From the preceding account of the company's situation, it should be obvious that Orion can be characterized as predominantly a dramatic company. Such companies often pursue inconsistent strategies and needlessly squander resources. By identifying the predominant organizational type, we became alert to a range of hitherto unobserved but frequently correlated behaviors. Although initially our attention was directed only to the most overt symptoms, our identification of the dramatic theme prepared us to look for others, essential for a final diagnosis. Paying attention to these deeper dynamics made us more aware and better prepared to undertake change.

We noticed how Pizzi centralized power and impulsively controlled too many divisions. We knew from previous experience that dramatic firms have great difficulty controlling operations because of their risky and dangerous policies. We also realized that in these firms there is frequently no competent second tier of managers to take care of operations. The more competent managers—those willing to express their own opinions—tend to leave.

In the Orion Corporation, we interviewed many very dependent executives who desired to be "nourished" and protected by the president from the turmoil around them. Many of them had complete faith in Pizzi's actions. Even when in doubt they would rationalize what their leader was doing. A critical stance was rare. Those who found Pizzi's style difficult to take conformed, let themselves be victimized, or left the company.

We also noted another typical feature of the dramatic style: Pizzi's feelings about his subordinates could change very quickly. Small incidents tended to cause a shift in attitude—a manager could be a hero one day and a villain the next. Pizzi's relatonships with his staff assistant or his vice-president of operations were cases in point.

## What to Recommend?

Our first, most important task was to establish a working alliance with the president. Given the political realities at Orion, this concern overrode all others. Without support from Pizzi we could do nothing. In most interventions, this is the greatest hurdle. Neurotic leaders who are unwilling to cooperate—and Pizzi had shown tremendous unwillingness in the past to be cooperative with other consultants—prevent implementation of even the soundest recommendations.

To gain support from Pizzi we tried building on his tendency to temporarily "idealize" what we as consultants could do for him. We realized from past experience this would only serve us initially, helping to establish a basis for a working relationship. We knew, too, that Pizzi had a very limited tolerance for frustration. In fact, too much insight into what made him tick or into his responsibility for the pressing problems of the firm might actually arrest the change process, making him too upset to continue. We would then be dismissed like the consultants who had come before us. Thus the timing of our interventions was critical.

But we had one thing going for us: Orion was now in the red, undeniably, and Pizzi had to do something. Deeply concerned about the demands being made on him by Orion's banks, he realized his power was being threatened. So he was already motivated to try to change as we approached him with our recommendations. Given the emotional investment he had in the company, its potential loss became the wedge we could use in the change process.

Outside pressure can elicit cooperation and self-examination. Someone outside the organization, especially with influence or outright control over the firm, will have the greatest effect. The experience of powerless whistle blowers has been generally dismal. Although alerting everyone to a crisis may be honorable and logical, it often ends in dressing down or dismissal.

Therefore, parties from the outside, with at least an equal footing to the CEO, must work for change. A board of directors, for example. The board's job (unfortunately not often enough taken) is to raise issues with its CEO, make subtle suggestions for change, and then, if necessary, demand change.

A bank can also be very useful, requiring new controls, new policies, and special audits in return for continued lines of credit. In Pizzi's case, the banks levied very useful "outside pressure."

In the absence of such pressures, change is hard to achieve.

After completing our organizational audit, we scheduled a number of problem-solving sessions with Pizzi in which we included all of his key executives. We asked Pizzi first what he saw as the company's main strengths.

"Well, we're very strong on product quality and durability," he began, "and our distribution system is top-rate. And I'd say our reputation in the box field is one of reliability and consistency."

We asked the executives if they concurred and, after some discussion, most said they did. We then asked Pizzi, the managers, everyone, to create a realistic plan for the future, keeping in mind these agreed-upon distinctive competences. We asked for suggestions concerning cost cutting, consolidation, and margin-building. The managers threw themselves into the task, and soon creative ideas began to emerge. The problems were made implicit by discussing solutions—and encouraging sensible suggestions. When it was over, the process of working through Orion's problems in this more open setting seemed to boost Pizzi's key executives to points of much higher self-confidence. They began expressing more opinions, gently questioning, for the first time, the president's viewpoint.

We observed Pizzi, too, gradually becoming more comfortable with the idea of open discussion and joint, participatory decision-making. Then, to ensure continued motivation to change, we explored with Pizzi a few extreme possibilities. At opportune times we exaggerated what could happen to the company if certain actions were not quickly taken. Occasionally we confessed to a sense of pessimism about our being able to effect any kind of constructive change. "One fear we have is of failing like the consultants before us," we said. "Your predicament at Orion just might be too much for us to handle." Then we asked Pizzi point-blank, "How prepared are you for bad news? Not everything we've learned here about your company is very pretty." In effect, we were daring him to prove us wrong, to resist our gloomy predictions. We hoped his drive and energy, combined with his fears of his bankers, would make him rise to the occasion.

To our great delight, that's exactly what began to happen. Gradually Pizzi became aware of his own role in creating the problems at Orion. But we had to monitor his reactions very carefully so as not to overload him. Too much negative feedback will sometimes drive a neurotic right back to where he began. So initially, we continued to emphasize the strengths of the company and Pizzi's important role in creating them. We had to introduce only small doses of insight in explaining problems.

During our consultations with neurotic companies, we consider two approaches: the "Worst-Case Scenario" and the "Sandwich."

### The Worst-Case Scenario

The worst-case scenario approach hits the CEO right over the head by telling him everything you've found out.

"You're going to lose it all, your management team is planning to quit on you, the bank is planning to freeze your assets, and the board is pissed!" When the situation is at its most critical, when there is not much time, and there is a reasonable chance the CEO is strong enough, and/or open enough, you use the worst-case scenario. If the CEO's sense of reality is too far gone, however, this approach may backfire. Unwilling to face the situation, defensive processes may come to the fore.

### The Sandwich

The second approach we use more frequently. With the sandwich method, you first present good news (one slice of bread), then bad news (the fixings), then more good news (second piece of bread). Maybe you even offer the CEO three or four sandwiches, a Dagwood-like variation. Hopefully, this easy-hard-easy combination cushions any devastating blow and preserves a shaky neurotic leader's self-esteem and willingness to go on with our recommendations. The introduction of humor at the same time can be an additional facilitating factor.

So one day we offered Doug Pizzi a "sandwich." In the course of our serving it, the president became more aware of how his behavior affected the operations of his company, and surprisingly amenable to various structural changes aimed at counteracting his disruptive style. Then we proposed avenues for cost cutting, consolidation, and plant usage, new control systems for Orion, and strategic business units that might better track performance. Criteria were established for the selection, promotion, and placement of personnel and the clearer allocation of responsibility.

After careful analysis of Orion's markets and competition, Pizzi was persuaded to discontinue three money-losing divisions. Given the company's dire financial straits, the divisions were no longer economically feasible. One division was pruned and merged, two others sold entirely. Part of the unused production facilities were then leased out to reduce overhead costs.

The joint meetings of Pizzi, his executives, and ourselves engineered much support for these measures. Indeed, as we had hoped, it became difficult to know who first suggested them. In tentatively questioning some of Pizzi's (or our own) recommendations at the now-regular planning sessions, key executives acquired a more critical attitude. Divergent comments and constructive criticism from managers were becoming more acceptable.

At post mortems of these meetings with the president, we pointed out the benefits of this approach of constructive engagement and the vital role he had to play. Gradually Pizzi's increased confidence and improved knowledge of himself made him more accepting of dissent and less inclined to look for scapegoats. In addition, two new managers joined the company, adding to the development of a more mixed corporate culture.

Pizzi himself, in fact, within six months of the initial common planning session, began to change. His self-confidence was heightened so that he no longer seemed to need to act out so much or make himself the center of attention. He was much more at ease with his key executives, too, and far less inclined to blame them for the company's troubles.

"I'm delegating more than ever in my life," he bragged one day, "I let my people manage now and I can see the value in letting a lot of the responsibility go. It certainly makes my life easier. I think I'm beginning to be more trusting!"

To ensure that things stayed on track we met with the key executives first on a weekly and later on a monthly basis for a deliberately fixed period to avoid drawn-out dependency reactions. Such meetings were formalized through a planning and operations committee whose main objectives were to implement the new organization structure, review policy, plan strategy, and assess performance. This was not an easy project, however. Several times we almost gave up, expecting Pizzi to throw us out. Though his insight into his dramatic behavior was steadily helping him to change, he had many relapses.

In fact, over a year went by until strategy became well enough focused and responsibilities sufficiently defined that some complementarity finally existed among Orion's divisions. Not insignificantly, Orion is also back in the black.

We do not wish to pretend, however, that Pizzi underwent a tremendous metamorphosis and changed his style completely. To this day his flair for the dramatic continues. But this is, in many ways, fortunate. It was, after all, Pizzi's vision and initiative that originally pushed Orion over the sales plateau it had been on for such a long time.

By giving Pizzi insight into how his personality had affected his organization we only removed some of his excesses or at least their worst manifestations. We also made him more conscious of the need for controlled and planned change, but without extinguishing his adventurer's spirit.

## Reacting to Catastrophe

Putting companies and neurotic executives "on the couch" does not so much eliminate neurotic styles as reduce the damage they do. The truth is that a compulsive, dramatic, or suspicious executive will probably always be just that, though if such leaders become aware of neurotic tendencies, containment and rechanneling can take place. Depressives, in organizations however, usually have a more formidable task. They have to change—otherwise, not much can be accomplished. Like the depressive, the detached executive needs to get out of his or her from behind the closed office and get moving. Some form of shock treatment may be needed so that there is pain in the system.

Gerald Trautman, a top executive at Greyhound for fifteen years, and a man whom we would characterize as "detached" faced a catastrophe near the end of his tenure. In 1978, faced with a barrage of complaints and financial problems, Trautman finally stepped out of his sanctum and began touring the bus routes, dropping in on Greyhound's sources of unrest, such as maintenance garages and ticket terminals, and even riding the company's buses. Opening himself up to all kinds of information, he encountered tales of equipment breakdowns, plugged-up washrooms, security bungles, and bureaucratic nightmares.

"It was all beginning to add up to a pretty bad picture," he remarked later. "I really got an earful."[2] Added Frank Najeotte, Trautman's second in command: "It had gotten to a point where an irate passenger with a complicated problem in some eastern city often had to wait for messages to go back and forth to headquarters [in Phoenix] in order to have it resolved. We put a stop to that."[3]

Trautman and Najeotte responded to these problems immediately. They expanded decision-making authority in the field and increased staffing everywhere. They hired police officers to patrol terminals, and they saw that maintenance received the highest priority for the first time in years. As a result, the next year, 1979, bus breakdowns declined by a third, while total revenues reached their highest mark since 1974. Trautman's willingness to become more involved improved matters substantially. His previous detached style, however, had prevented him from even knowing of his company's problems.

## Self-help: Seven Steps to Prevention

As we have indicated, pain in the system—both inside and out—can create momentum for change. But because of "character armor"—the tenacity of personality and patterns of behavior to resist change—sometimes the only way to truly transform an organization is to replace key executives. Frequently personalities cannot change, and where they are the sources of problems in organizations, difficulties will last as long as the responsible executive's tenure.

Dismissal, however, is a last resort. Wise executives should engage in preventive maintenance first, searching for ways to make it unlikely a company will run to dangerous extremes. Once firms reach these extremes, change is far more difficult.

Most executives do not possess sufficient reflective capacity to stand back and take stock of their actions without the aid of consultants. Given their power in the system, they can freely hang on to configurated and misleading notions. But there are methods of self-help available, especially if executives are open to them. The following are our seven steps to prevention of neurotic management styles: strategic ambiguity, organic designs, organizational renewal, innovative human resource management practices, corporate slack, incentives and rewards, and external agents. But these are not panaceas and must be used with caution. They have to be tailored to the needs of the specific organization.

### Strategic Ambiguity

We cannot overemphasize the importance of declaring a company's mission and core values (i.e., excellence, growth, service, risk taking, etc.) At the same time, these declarations must never be made exhaustive or rigid. The various components of strategy must allow a certain amount of interpretive discretion.

## "Organic" Designs

"Ad-hocracies" are organizational forms that foster teamwork and enhance adaptability. They include such devices as temporary task forces, product groups, project teams, networking systems, and participative management. "Skunkworks," (facilities set apart from the rest of the corporation) and "bootleg" projects (activities done inofficially or tolerated semiofficially) also can boost creativity and flexibility. Planned personnel rotation, too, helps break routine patterns and facilitates introduction of new ideas.

Though trendy structural designs do not in themselves foster collaboration and a sense of involvement, there is some evidence that structures that are "flat" do. It seems that power in such structures tends to reside in those with the greatest expertise, encouraging the exploration of new ideas. A lateral communication results, leading to cross-fertilization and the development of nondogmatic consensus.

Open, horizontal communication systems stress frequent and informal contact and contribute to the free flow of information and a more felicitous resolution of conflict. Distinctions in rank should be kept at a minimum. The wide distribution of power and authority can breed creativity; participation, instead, breeds individual initiative.

But such organizational changes are not likely to be easily accepted given the tendency of some CEOs to retain power and control. Also, more authoritarian, bureaucratic structures actually do quite well in stable industries: They are certainly much more efficient than the flexible forms.

But always remember that their rigidity can create enormous problems when change is necessary.

## Self-Renewal

Adaptive organizations have organizational climates that stress flexibility. To bring this about, regular reviews are needed of organizational policies and management practices, continual "audits" of leadership, culture, strategy, and structure.

Managers must continually ask if these are still valid under new circumstances. Such reviews should create a climate of constant learning at the organizational, departmental, and individual levels. Such learning is not simply a process of digesting new facts, but of developing an investigative, questioning attitude, of "learning how to learn".[4] This obviously occurs best in an atmosphere of openness and trust.

## Innovative Human Resource Management Practices

An organization should tolerate, indeed encourage, eccentricities among its employees. Acceptance of the unorthodox boosts the perceived range of strategic options and opportunities. Thus sometimes it will be useful to assign nonspecialists to specific problems and use devil's advocates to stir up discussion. The fresh ideas that result may go far in combatting rigidity. In contrast, selection of CEO "clones" as powerful managers is one sure way to guarantee corporate myopia and a deadening uniformity in policies, strategies, and management practices.

An organization's members should also engage in continual reexamination of informal company rules and mores. Such reviews tend to prevent employees from being molded into the same profile. A certain amount of nonconformity is necessary for creativity, adaptivity, and flexibility.

It is, however, important to stress that these latter characteristics might not always be desirable in an organization.

One would expect armies of flexible noncomformists to win few military battles.

## Corporate Slack

Slack, excess resources such as funds, materials, time, space, and staff, enable members of the organization to engage in activities that are not possible when working under tight constraints. Although generally outside a manager's control—due to economic and/or industrial circumstances—some administrative slack is needed to take advantage of emerging opportunities.

Where possible, slack should be gathered during periods of prosperity, since it is all but impossible to engage in creative activity while firefighting.

Exclusive concern with short-term efficiency and productivity can obliterate the opportunity for creativity and strategic reorientation to take advantage of shifting markets. Among the questions that the organizational leadership should ask are: Is there slack time available for deliberations about strategy, goods, markets, and personnel policies? Or is the organizational culture one in which firefighting prevails? Is there discretionary spending authority at lower levels for innovative projects? Does each budget have some unplanned discretionary funds?

## Incentives and Rewards

Some incentives and reward systems discourage risk-taking, allowing only the safe, the tried and true. But to create an adaptive organization one must encourage risk-taking. "Intrapreneurship," that is, pioneering, grass roots, innovative entrepreneurship within the setting of larger companies, may be one way to do this. In such situations executives may be given a stake in their firm via profit sharing and stock options.

Naturally, constant renewal requires a CEO with confidence and trust in the members of the organization. Also, renewal may negate the departmental, bureaucratic "territorial" imperative: New ideas are not necessarily tied to specific organizational boundaries.

Employees must also be encouraged to take chances and to make mistakes, and the organization must be prepared to accept failures. Premature criticism and meddling can destroy even the best idea. Of course, this philosophy can be taken too far. Risk-taking should not turn the firm into a dramatic organization.

## External Agents of Change

Individuals from outside the organization possess a very different frame of reference than that of the employees. Consultants, for example, can thus play an important role as critics, appraisors and catalysts for change.

But consultants hired to do a quick assignment are unlikely to have enough time to discern the underlying sources of difficulties in an organization. Therefore, it is advisable to engage those who can develop a long term relationship with the organization. The company should, moreover, try to employ consultants who value frankness in feedback above contract security. Some internal consultants will also fit this bill. The constant threat, of course, is that the honest critic will be discharged.

Other possible agents of change: external directors (appointed mainly for their knowledge and breadth of experience), and bankers.

Participation in outside training groups may also be useful as these provide a nonthreatening environment in which executives can discuss working experiences with professionals who have a broad knowledge of different organizational cultures and management styles. This tends to create better understanding of organizational strategies for change.

Chapter Ten

# Conclusion

Those who cannot remember the past are condemned to repeat it.

George Santayana

**P**hilosophers over the ages have pronounced that people—and their leaders—are ruled chiefly by passion, not reason. In life, it is thought, one has to choose between *action* and *reflection*. To combine these two orientations seems not only difficult, but, at times, a gross contradiction.

Too often the problems in the unsuccessful organizations come about because this elusive, precarious, and even somewhat contradictory balance between action and reflection has been lost. Many times top executives get stuck in a specific scenario, a certain point of view and way of behaving, from which they are unable to disentangle themselves.

Their myopic view of the world encourages a wish for more of the same. The only options they see as sensible are those repetitive, if meaningless, management routines that now take on almost ritualistic qualities. Obsessions motivate

195

a need to control; fears breed suspicion; dramatic behaviors lead to grandiosity. And so it goes.

Many of the executives cited in the preceding chapters lost sight of what they were doing and found it difficult to change. Tenaciously they held fast to archaic, unhealthy, counterproductive activities that had once proved effective or pleasant for them, but that now no longer seemed to be working.

The result? A general ossifying of the organization. The capacity for critical thinking and reflection disappeared. Perhaps Goethe had this in mind when he said: "Know thyself? If I knew myself, I'd run away."

If you have recognized yourself, or your organization, in one of our five neurotic types, do not be alarmed. In fact, many of our psychological patterns are very much a part of most people's daily lives. Moreover, human behavior is usually characterized by a mixture of these styles, as are many organizations. We probably all share elements of many of the styles, each of which tends to become more pronounced under varying circumstances.

There is cause for concern only if one specific neurotic style takes over and consistently dominates all aspects of an organization's life. When this happens, it can all but completely cancel out the company's effectiveness.

For the purpose of exposition, we focused mainly on characteristics in "pure" constellations when discussing our five neurotic management types. But, as we pointed out, clinical pictures are often far more complicated and "pure" types are relatively rare. Combinations or mixtures are far more common.

Although the personality of a top manager can vitally influence an organization, we also argue that this will not necessarily rule out a reverse relationship. A failing organization rife with disappointment can surely make a leader depressed. And a series of vicious threats from the competition may lead to corporate paranoia. Consider the success, too, of a bold expansion program: Quite possibly more dramatic behavior on the part of the orchestrating CEO will follow. Certainly we do not subscribe to simple cause-and-effect relationships—mutual causation is the rule.

Before closing, we acknowledge, too, the healthy "hybrid" organization. Here the weaknesses endemic to a certain neurotic style are cancelled out by the strengths of another. Consider these combinations of three of our types— dramatic, compulsive, and suspicious: The energy and innovation of the dramatic can often be complemented by the caution and conservativeness of the suspicious. Or the attention to detail of the compulsive organization can offset the excess of the dramatic.

But there are some ill-fated hybrids, too: Compulsive-depressive or detached-depressive combinations usually make for leadership vacuums so profound, and an organization so political and fragmented, that an adaptive strategy is not likely to emerge.

Our approach to organizational diagnosis has a number of advantages. It is marked, we believe, by its depth, comprehensiveness, and psychological bent. Our framework is holistic, searching out common configurations, themes, or *gestalts* as characterized by CEO personalities, cultures, structures, and strategies. We avoid the confusion of the "one-thing-at-a-time" approach so common in typical modern organizational analysis.[1] In our work, connections and central unifying characteristics which occur repeatedly are examined and emphasized.

Also, individuals are seen as total persons as we search for major adaptive styles that motivate and characterize much of their behavior. We eschew the narrow schemes of emotion or cognition that divide personalities into separate, unrelated traits. We believe strongly that reality just isn't built that way.

By discussing leaders in terms of our five troubled styles, we integrate diverse aspects of personality into single coordinated configurations. Also, our framework identifies many of the psychological roots of strategic, structural, and cultural problems in organizations. Mere "symptom suppression" —the implementation of a new information system, for example—is unlikely to improve the long-term health of an organization. Such methods will not be used properly under the wrong ideology, by the wrong culture, or within the wrong structure. One must wake up to the deeper dynamics in organizations and find the root causes of problems as they may be found in the CEO's personality and the corporate culture.

The identification of specific neurotic styles and organizational types may alert managers to a range of as yet unobserved but frequently correlated behaviors. The capacity to suggest characteristics beyond the immediately observable gives value to our emphasis on configurations. This eases the work of the organizational detective, or at least helps him or her to ask better questions.

## Miracle Cures

Many years of hard experience and setbacks have taught us to distrust Instant-Change panaceas. That occasional "miracle cure" all too often deteriorates into a temporary and useless expedient. Many of the forces in organizations wedge too deeply inside the company's psychic walls, resisting quick solutions. All too often these forces illustrate long-standing, deeply ingrained ways of perception and action on the part of coalitions of the more powerful members of the organization. Such patterns are very hard to alter, even when their dire consequences seem obvious to everyone looking in from the outside.

Change often demands a major intervention process. Even counterproductive organizations possess a certain integrity, an ability to reinforce weaknesses and negative traits and bolster the whole. Because of this, small changes will do very little good. In general, only a new alignment of elements, a quantum change, can turn a firm around.[2] Piece-meal, incremental changes will be too limited, too inconsistent with the organization's balance, to do any good.

Only a disposition toward self-discovery and exploration can provide managers (and consultants) with insight into an organization's counterproductive behavior. And only in this way can a new, effective configuration evolve, one in which the individual pieces complement each other, one that is in tune with the market. What has become obvious to us is that leaders in the future, apart from having basic technical competence and a propensity for action, need to pay far more attention to their own interior processes, their own inner needs, their own capacity for such things as honest self-reflection and true empathy. This departs from traditional management settings, where rote, uncritical or even hyperactive behavior is more the rule.

In Chinese calligraphy the sign for change combines the symbols for danger and opportunity. We live today in a world of accelerating change that requires more and more adaptability. More than ever, inflexibility endangers corporate survival. In many of our case examples, the sources of the problems were groupthink, rigidity, and insularity, often caused by ossified leadership.

Leadership of the future will need to combine action with reflection and passion with reason. Creative leaders need not only to articulate and enact goals to inspire their followers, they must also pay attention to their own inner worlds to retain an attitude of reflection, objectivity, and inquiry. They need to get more in touch with their fantasies, fears, needs, and blind spots, using this knowledge as best they can to avoid rigid or counterproductive behavior.[3] As the French statesman de Tocqueville once said: "We succeed in enterprises which demand the positive qualities we possess, but we excel in those which can also make use of our defects."

# Notes

## Introduction

## Chapter 1: Organizations in Crisis

1. William B. Harris, "Litton Shoots for the Moon," *Fortune*, April 1958, p. 114; see also Carl Rieser, "When the Crowd Goes One Way Litton Goes the Other," *Fortune*, May 1963, p. 115; and Litton Industries Inc., AR, BR, C, in Edmund P. Learned, C. Roland Christensen, Kenneth R. Andrews, and William D. Guth, *Business Policy: Text and Cases*, rev. ed. (Homewood, Ill.: Richard D. Irwin, 1969), pp. 808–57.
2. Rieser, "When the Crowd," p. 228; and William S. Rukeyser, "Litton Down to Earth," *Fortune*, April 1968, p. 140.
3. Rieser, "When the Crowd," p. 117.
4. Rukeyser, "Litton Down to Earth," p. 139.
5. *The Economist*, April 13, 1968, p. 71.
6. "The Model Conglomerate Tries to Be an Operating Company," *Business Week*, December 1, 1973, p. 67.
7. Rieser, "When the Crowd," p. 186.
8. *The Economist*, April 13, 1968, p. 71.
9. Rieser, "When the Crowd," p. 222.
10. Ibid. p. 225.
11. Rukeyser, "Litton Down to Earth," p. 186.
12. Thoman O'Hanlon, "A Rejuvenated Litton Is Once Again Off to the Races," *Fortune*, October 8, 1979, p. 158.
13. See Anne Jardim, *The First Henry Ford: A Study in Personality and Business Leadership* (Cambridge, Mass: MIT Press, 1970).

201

14. Lally Weymouth, "Tycoon: The Saga of Henry Ford II," *New York Times Magazine*, March 5, 1978, p. 17.
15. Ibid. p. 17, 60.
16. Ibid. p. 60.
17. Ibid. p. 61.
18. Ibid. p. 60, 61.
19. Ibid. p. 61.

## Chapter 2: The Dramatic Organization

1. Charles Raw, Bruce Page, and Godfrey Hodgson, *Do You Sincerely Want to Be Rich?* (New York: Viking, 1971), p. 4.
2. Ibid. p. 8.
3. Robert Ball, "Bernie Cornfeld: The Salesman Who Believed Himself," *Fortune*, September 1970, p. 138.
4. Phillip L. Zweig, *Belly Up: The Collapse of the Penn Square Bank* (New York: Crown, 1985).
5. Roy Rowen, "The Swinger Who Broke Penn Square Bank," *Fortune*, August 23, 1982, p. 123.
6. Ibid.
7. Ibid.
8. See Mark Singer, *Funny Money* (New York: Alfred A. Knopf, 1985).
9. Ibid.
10. Raw et al., *Do You Sincerely Want to Be Rich?*, pp. 20–21.
11. Robert A. Hutchison, "The Looting of 10S," *Fortune*, March 5, 1973.
12. Ann M. Morrison, "How De Lorean Dashed His Dream," *Fortune*, May 3, 1982, p. 150.
13. See J. Patrick Wright, *On a Clear Day You Can See General Motors* (New York: Avon Books, 1984); Gail Sheehy, *Passages* (New York: Bantam Books, 1977); and Hillel Levin, *Grand Delusions* (New York: Viking, 1983).
14. Bro Uttal, "Itel's Lavish Living," *Fortune*, October 8, 1979, p. 113.
15. Ibid. p. 108.
16. Ibid. p. 116.
17. "Insider Looming over Itel," *Business Week*, January 28, 1985.
18. Raw et al., *Do You Sincerely Want to Be Rich?*, p. 57.
19. Ibid. pp. 59–60.
20. Morrison, "How De Lorean Dashed His Dream," p. 142.
21. Gwen Kinkead, "Trouble in D. K. Ludwig's Jungle," *Fortune*, April 20, 1981, p. 106.
22. Ibid. p. 107.

23. Louis Kraar, "Roy Ash Is Having Fun At Addressogrief-Multigrief," *Fortune*, February 27, 1978, p. 52.
24. Susie Gharbi Nazem, "How Roy Ash Got Burned," *Fortune*, April 6, 1981, p. 72.
25. Ibid. p. 71.
26. Alred P. Sloan, Jr., *My Years with General Motors* (New York: MacFadden Books, 1965), p. 26.
27. Ibid. p. 26.
28. Stephen J. Sansweet, "Armand Hammer Is Gradually Loosening Control at Occidental," *Wall Street Journal*, May 12, 1978, p. 1. See also Gwen Kinkead, "Armand Hammer's Costly Dreams," *Fortune*, November 26, 1984; and Andrew Duncan, "Dream of a Rich, Powerful Man: Peace and a Cure for Cancer," *Montreal Gazette*, May 7, 1986, p. 1; and Armand Hammer with Neil Lyndon, *Hammer* (New York: G. P. Putnam's Sons, 1987).
29. Peter W. Bernstein, "Armand Hammer's Other Collection," *Fortune*, September 8, 1980, p. 48.

## Chapter 3: The Suspicious Organization

1. See Manfred F. R. Kets de Vries and Joel Uchenick, "J. Edgar Hoover and the FBI," Case Study, McGill University, Faculty of Management, 1979; see also Frederick L. Collins, *The FBI in Peace and War* (New York: Putnam, 1943); Don Whitehead, *The FBI Story: A Report to the People* (New York: Random House, 1956); Hans Messick, *John Edgar Hoover: An Inquiry into the Life and Times of John Edgar Hoover and His Relationship to the Continuing Partnership of Crime, Business and Politics* (New York: David McKay, 1972); Sanford Ungar, *FBI* (Boston: Atlantic Monthly Press, 1975); Joseph L. Schott, *No Left Turns* (New York: Praeger, 1975); Neil J. Welch and David W. Marston, *Inside Hoover's FBI: The Top Field Chief Reports* (Garden City, N.Y.: Doubleday, 1984); and Richard Gid Powers, *Secrecy and Power: The Life of J. Edgar Hoover* (New York: Free Press, 1987).
2. Schott, *No Left Turns*, p. 28.
3. Ibid. pp. 149–50.
4. Ibid. p. 59.
5. See International Telephone and Telegraph Corporation (A & B) 1-483-105, Harvard Business School Case, President and Fellows of Harvard College, 1983.
6. Stanley H. Brown, "How One Man Can Move a Corporate Mountain," *Fortune*, July 1, 1966, p. 83.
7. Harold Geneen and Alvin Moscow, *Managing* (Garden City, N.Y.: Doubleday, 1984), pp. 96–99.

8. Ibid. Chapter 4.
9. Collins, *The FBI in Peace and War*, p. ix.
10. Ann Crittenden, "The Hunt Brothers: How They Deal," *New York Times*, January 6, 1980.
11. Roy Rowan, "A Hunt Crony Tells All," *Fortune*, June 30, 1980, p. 60.
12. Whitehead, *The FBI Story*, p. 119.
13. Wilfred R. Bion, *Experiences in Groups* (New York: Ballantine, 1961).
14. Schott, *No Left Turns*, pp. 5–6.
15. Ungar, *FBI*, p. 262.
16. Joe Klein, "Labor Pains," *New York*, March 25, 1985, p. 47.
17. Ibid. p. 44.
18. Lee Iacocca with William Novak, *Iacocca: An Autobiography* (New York, Bantam Books, 1984), p. 111.
19. Ibid. p. 127.
20. Schott, *No Left Turns*, pp. 12–13.
21. Ibid. p. 22.
22. Crittenden, "The Hunt Brothers," p. 4.
23. Ibid. p. 4.
24. Richard Nixon, *The Memoirs of Richard Nixon* (New York: Grosset and Dunlap, 1981), pp. 589–99.
25. Geoffrey Colvin, "The De-Geneening of ITT," *Fortune*, January 11, 1982, p. 34.

## Chapter 4: The Detached Organization

1. Michael Moritz and Barrett Seaman, *Going for Broke* (Garden City: N.Y.: Doubleday, 1981), p. 85.
2. Peter J. Schuyten, "Chrysler Goes for Broke," *Fortune*, June 19, 1978, p. 55.
3. Moritz and Seaman, *Going for Broke*, p. 83.
4. Schuyten, "Chrysler Goes for Broke," p. 55.
5. Moritz and Seaman, *Going for Broke*, p. 85.
6. Ibid. p. 86.
7. Ibid. p. 85.
8. American Psychiatric Association, *Diagnostic and Statistical Manual of Mental Disorders, DSM-III* (Washington, D.C., 1982).
9. Moritz and Seaman, *Going for Broke*, p. 85.
10. Moritz and Seaman, *Going for Broke*, p. 86.
11. Ibid. p. 85.
12. Charles J. V. Murphey and T. A. Wise, "The Problem of Howard Hughes," *Fortune*, January 1959, p. 81. See also Donald L. Barlett and James B. Steele, *Empire: The Life, Legend and Madness of*

*Howard Hughes* (New York: Norton, 1979); see also James Phelan, *Howard Hughes: The Hidden Years* (New York: Random House, 1976).

13. Gwen Kinkead, "Sotheby's Lost Art: Management," *Fortune*, May 31, 1982, p. 127.
14. Ibid.
15. Jeffrey Hogrefe, *Wholly Unacceptable* (New York: Morrow, 1986).
16. Kinkead, "Southeby's Lost Art: Management," p. 127.
17. Ibid. p. 128.
18. Ibid.
19. Lisa Winkler, "The New Yankee Influence Comes to Sotheby's," *International Management*, November 1983; see also Hogrefe, *Wholly Unacceptable*.
20. "Raadgevend Bureau Ir. B. W. Berenschot NV (A-I)," in C. Roland Christensen, Kenneth R. Andrews, and Joseph L. Bower, *Business Policy: Text and Cases*, 3rd ed. (Homewood, Ill: Richard D. Irwin, 1973), p. 547.
21. Philip Siekman, "Belgium's Muscle-Bound Giant," *Fortune*, February 1969.
22. Ibid. p. 138.
23. Alexander Stuart, "Greyhound Gets Ready for a New Driver," *Fortune*, December 15, 1980, p. 59.
24. Ibid.
25. Siekman, "Belgium's Muscle-Bound Giant," p. 100.
26. *Wall Street Journal*, November 28, 1984.
27. Katrine Ames, "Beverly in Bloom," *Savvy*, May 1987.

## Chapter 5: The Depressive Organization

1. Stanley Brown, "The Hidden Appeal of Allis-Chalmers," *Fortune*, November 1967, p. 157.
2. Rush Loving, Jr., "How a Hotelman Got the Best Out of United Airlines," *Fortune*, March 1972, p. 73.
3. Ibid.
4. Roger Beardwood, "Melville Draws a Bead on the $50-Billion Fashion Market," *Fortune*, December 1969.
5. Loving, "How a Hotelman," p. 77.
6. Ibid.
7. "Problems in Walt Disney's Magic Kingdom," *Business Week*, March 12, 1984; Myron Magnet, "No More Mickey Mouse at Disney," *Fortune*, December 10, 1984; "Disney's Magic," *Business Week*, March 4, 1987. See also John Taylor, *Storming the Magic Kingdom* (New York: Alfred A. Knopf, 1987.

8. Aljean Harmetz, "Disney Hopes Eisner Can Wake Sleeping Beauty," *New York Times*, October 17, 1984, p. C20.
9. Mary Bralove, "Tough Turnaround: Now Only No 2, A&P Is Trying Harder—But Harder Enough?", *Wall Street Journal*, September 19, 1974, p. 1.
10. Ibid.; see also Bill Saporito, "Just How Good Is the Great A&P," *Fortune*, March 16, 1987.

## Chapter 6: The Compulsive Organization

1. Hugh D. Menzies, "The Ten Toughest Bosses," *Fortune*, April 21, 1980.
2. *Business Week*, June 28, 1976, p. 90.
3. Ibid. p. 93.
4. Sewell Lee Avery, Harvard Business School Case, SPM 8, President and Fellows of Harvard College, 1969.
5. Irwin Ross, "The Private Turbulence at Eastern Airlines," *Fortune*, July 1964.
6. David Blum, "The Road to Ishtar," *New York*, March 16, 1987, p. 41.
7. Susan Fraker, "How DEC Got Decked," *Fortune*, December 12, 1983, p. 84.
8. Ibid. p. 88.
9. Ibid. p. 92.
10. *Life*, May 2, 1949.
11. George Brown, "Reminiscences, pp. 110–11, Ford Archives.
12. Bro Uttal, "Texas Instruments Regroups," *Fortune*, August 9, 1982, p. 44.
13. Ibid.
14. Brian O'Reilly, "Texas Instruments: New Boss, Big Job," *Fortune*, July 8, 1985, p. 37.
15. Uttal, "Texas Instruments Regroups," p. 44.
16. Ibid.
17. *Fortune*, May 1946, p. 112.
18. Ibid.
19. "Problems in Walt Disney's Magic Kingdom," p. 50; see also "Disney's Magic" and Taylor, *Storming the Magic Kingdom*.
20. Alden Whitman, "DeWitt Wallace, Founder of Reader's Digest Is Dead," *New York Times*, April 1, 1981.
21. Alex S. Jones, "At Reader's Digest, a Fight over Philosophy," *New York Times*, June 1, 1984, p. D3.
22. Edwin McDowell, "Reader's Digest: Down to Business," *International Herald Tribune*, February 13, 1986, pp. 11, 15.
23. Ross, "The Private Turbulence," p. 173.

24. Ibid. p. 174.
25. Fraker, "How DEC Got Decked."
26. Bro Uttal, "Texas Instruments Wrestles with the Consumer Market," *Fortune*, December 3, 1979.
27. Uttal, "Texas Instruments Regroups," p. 42.
28. Ross, "The Private Turbulence," p. 173.
29. *Wall Street Journal*, January 23, 1985; see also Alan Piper, "Breaking the Multinational Mould: How DEC Snuggled Up to Its Customers," *International Management*, November 1985, pp. 44–48; David E. Sanger, "Digital Revives on Its PC Strategy, *International Herald Tribune*, September 6–7, 1986, pp. 13, 17.

## Chapter 7: Playing Organizational Detective

1. Arthur Conan Doyle, "The Sign of the Four," *The Complete Sherlock Holmes*, Vol. 1 (New York: Doubleday, 1930), pp. 91–93.
2. See Manfred F. R. Kets de Vries, "Solving Mysteries: Playing Organizational Detective," Harvard Business School Technical note, 0-485-001, Presidents and Fellows of Harvard College, 1984; see also Manfred F. R. Kets de Vries and Danny Miller, "Interpreting Organizational Text," *Journal of Management Studies*, vol. 24, no. 3, May 1987 pp. 233–48.

## Chapter 8: Why Some Companies (and Their CEOs) Resist Change (and What to Do About It)

1. Otto Kernberg, *Object Relations Theory and Clinical Psychoanalysis* (New York: Jason Aronson, 1976).
2. Sheehy, *Passages*, pp. 398–404.
3. Erik H. Erikson, "Identity and the Life Cycle: Selected Papers," *Psychological Issues*, Monograph 1 (New York: International Universities Press, 1959).
4. Sigmund Freud, "Inhibitions, Symptoms and Anxiety," in James Strachey, ed., *The Standard Edition of the Complete Psychological Works of Sigmund Freud* Vol. 20, (London: The Hogarth Press and the Institute of Psychoanalysis, 1962).
5. See for example Manfred F. R. Kets de Vries, "Organizational Stress: A Call for Management Action," *Sloan Management Review*, Vol. 21, Fall 1979, pp. 3–14.
6. See Edgar H. Schein, *Organizational Culture and Leadership* (San Francisco; Jossey-Bass, 1985).
7. Gregory A. Patterson, "Bill Rodgers Hits the Wall," *Boston Globe*, April 19, 1987.

8. Alwin W. Goulder, *Patterns of Industrial Bureaucracy* (Glencoe, Ill: Free Press, 1954).
9. See Abraham Zaleznik and Manfred F. R. Kets de Vries, *Power and the Corporate Mind*, rev. ed. (Chicago: Bonus Books, 1985).
10. Sloan, *My Years with General Motors*, p. 26.
11. Alfred D. Chandler, Jr., *Strategy and Structure* (Garden City, N.Y.: Anchor Books, 1966), p. 191.
12. Colin, "The De-Geneening of ITT," p. 34.
13. See Michael Brody, "Cash Crunch at ITT," *Fortune*, February 18, 1985; "Rand Araskog Redeploys ITT: High Tech Is the Guiding Light," *International Management*, February 1985; and Leslie Wayne, "ITT: The Giant Slumbers," *New York Times*, July 1, 1984.
14. Bartlett and Steele, *Empire: The Life, Legend and Madness of Howard Hughes*, p. 193.
15. Gene Bylinsky, "Hughes Aircraft: The High-Flying Might Have Been," *Fortune*, April 1968, p. 103.
16. Loving, "How a Hotelman."
17. Bralove, "Tough Turnaround," p. 6.
18. Saporito, "Just How Good Is the Great A&P," p. 64.

## Chapter 9: Organizational Intervention: A Case Study

1. For a more detailed discussion of the dynamics of organizational intervention see Manfred F. R. Kets de Vries and Danny Miller, *The Neurotic Organization: Diagnosing and Changing Counterproductive Styles of Management* (San Francisco: Jossey-Bass, 1984); Kets de Vries, ed., *The Irrational Executive* (New York: International Universities Press, 1984); and Kets de Vries, *Prisoners of Leadership; Charting a Course Through the Corridors of Power* (forthcoming).
2. John Quint, "How Greyhound Made a U-Turn," *Fortune*, March 24, 1980, p. 139.
3. Ibid. p. 140.
4. Chris Argyris and Donald A. Schon, *Theory in Practice: Increasing Professional Effectiveness* (San Francisco: Jossey-Bass, 1974); and Donald A. Schon, *The Reflective Practitioner* (New York: Basic Books, 1983).

# Chapter 10: Conclusion

1. See Danny Miller and Peter H. Friesen, *Organizations: A Quantum View* (Englewood Cliffs, N.J.: Prentice-Hall, 1984) for a more detailed discussion of the approach of configuration and for the research methods used to isolate the pathological types of organizations discussed in this book. See also Danny Miller, "Towards a New Contingency Approach: The Search for Organizational Gestalts," *Journal of Management Studies*, Vol. 18, 1981, pp. 1–26, and Manfred F. R. Kets de Vries and Danny Miller, "Personality, Culture, and Organization," *Academy of Management Review*, Vol. 11, No. 2, 1986, pp. 266–79, for the advantages of the configural or gestalt approach to the study of organization.

2. The notion of quantum change is discussed by Miller and Friesen, *Organizations*; see also Miller and Friesen, "Structural Change and Performance: Quantum Versus Piecemeal Incremental Approaches," *Academy of Management Journal*, Vol. 25, 1982, pp. 867–92; and Miller, "Evolution and Revolution: A Quantum View of Structural Change in Organizations," *Journal of Management Studies*, Vol. 19, 1982, pp. 131–51.

3. Empirical support for the impact that the personality of a CEO can have on his or her organization is given by Danny Miller and Cornelia Droge, "Psychological and Traditional Determinants of Structure," *Administrative Science Quarterly*, Vol. 31, 1986, pp. 539–60; by Danny Miller and J. M. Toulouse, "CEO Personality and Corporate Strategy and Structure in Small Firms," *Management Science*, Vol. 32, 1986, pp. 1389–1409; and by Danny Miller, Manfred Kets de Vries, and J. M. Toulouse, "Top Executive Locus of Control and its Relationship to Strategy-making, Structure and Environment," *Academy of Management Journal*, Vol. 25, 1982, pp. 237–53.

# Index